Coming Up
Short
in a Tall World

Coming Up Short in a Tall World

Kel Groseclose

BETHANY HOUSE PUBLISHERS
MINNEAPOLIS, MINNESOTA 55438
A Division of Bethany Fellowship, Inc.

All Scripture verses are taken from the King James Version of the Bible unless otherwise marked.

Illustrated by Dwight Walles

Published by Bethany House Publishers
A Division of Bethany Fellowship, Inc.
6820 Auto Club Road, Minneapolis, MN 55438

Printed in the United States of America

Library of Congress Cataloging in Publication Data

Groseclose, Kel, 1940–
    Coming up short in a tall world.

    1. Parenting—Washington (State)—Anecdotes, facetiae, satire, etc. 2. Parenting—Religious aspects—Christianity. 3. Fathers—Washington (State)—Biography.
4. Groseclose, Kel, 1940–   I. Title.
HQ755.8.G75   1984   649'.125   84–11031
ISBN 0–87123–435–1 (pbk.)

Dedicated to Ellen, faithful wife and loving mother.
I appreciate her calming, steadfast presence, plus her cooking,
cleaning, taxiing, shopping, typing, and especially her hugs.

ABOUT THE AUTHOR

KEL GROSECLOSE is Associate Pastor of the First United Methodist Church in Wenatchee, Washington. The son of a Methodist pastor, he grew up in the Pacific Northwest and Alaska, graduating from the University of Puget Sound, Tacoma, Washington, with a B.A. in psychology and sociology. He holds the Bachelor of Sacred Theology degree from Boston University and is presently enrolled in the Doctor of Ministry program at San Francisco Theological Seminary, San Anselmo, California. Kel and his wife Ellen are the parents of six children: teenagers John, Stephen, Amy; and juniors Michael, Sara and David.

The author's first book is *Three-Speed Dad in a Ten-Speed World.*

PREFACE

"Pastor's panic" had struck. I felt as though someone had pulled the plug on my emotional reservoir and drained it dry. Even small, routine tasks which normally required little effort seemed monumental. I felt surrounded by demands, by "have-tos" and "musts," at a time when my energy dipstick registered below the ADD mark.

I was struggling to complete a sermon. It was probably a Saturday—Sunday morning loomed close on the calendar. Suddenly and undeservedly, I received the encouragement I so badly needed. It was the message of a father (David) to his son (Solomon), preparing him for the demands of constructing the Jerusalem Temple.

> Be strong and courageous *and get to work* [italics mine]. Don't be frightened by the size of the task, for the Lord my God is with you; he will not forsake you. He will see to it that everything is finished correctly (1 Chron. 28:20, TLB).

I also need such reassurance as I strive to be an effective parent. The size of the task is incredibly large and rather frightening. Ellen and I are responsible for raising our six children to age eighteen (and beyond); for providing their physical, intellectual, emotional, and spiritual needs; for comforting them, urging them forward, weeping and rejoicing with them.

The number of harmful, hurtful experiences awaiting them in the world is scary to contemplate. The wrong turns and dead ends they may encounter concern me. I worry about the kind of society they'll face as they begin their careers and start families of their own (if they so choose).

"Little" Johnny was a babe in arms only a short time ago. Now he's ready to graduate from high school, to register for the draft, to select a college. He's talking to Navy recruiters, sending off scholarship applications, and thinking seriously about possible professions.

It's a tall order to be a parent. I may soon be shorter than almost every one of my kids. In the meantime, I'm short on money, time and energy. But there's one important thing I'm not short on: God's help, His offer of wisdom and power. So I'm ready to get to work. I won't let the size of the task or my lack of size bother me. I have God's promise that Ellen's and my task of parenting will be finished correctly, even if not easily and certainly not perfectly.

Kel Groseclose
Wenatchee, Washington

TABLE OF CONTENTS

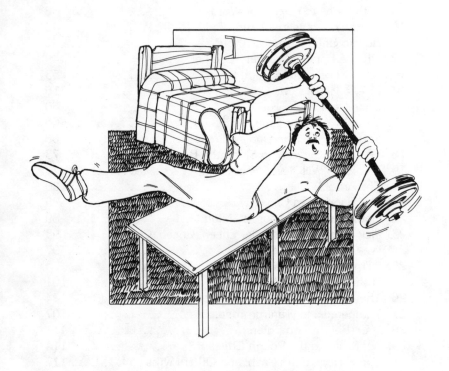

One

EAT YOUR HEART OUT, ARNOLD SCHWARZENEGGER

It was Friday, my usual day off. Michael would be hosting a slumber party that evening in honor of his eleventh birthday, so I decided to help Ellen ready the house for the onslaught.

Mistake number one: I entered fifteen-year-old Steve's room to do a little cleaning. I should have steered clear. Once inside, it became apparent that a little cleaning wouldn't go very far.

Halfway through the task, I sat down on his weight bench to catch my breath. It's actually my bench, but he's the one who's serious about using it. I eyed the weights resting on the rack and thought, *While I'm here, I might as well bench press that. I outweigh him by at least fifty pounds, so surely, I can lift what he can—easily.*

Mistake number two: I lay back on the bench, took the barbells off their resting place and lowered them to my chest. Breathing became more difficult. Slowly I began to lift. The higher I raised the bar, the more slowly it rose. I grunted and pushed for all I was worth, but I could not raise it high enough to set it back on the rack.

The weights began their inevitable descent, gaining speed as they came down against my chest. Breathing was now even more difficult. At least the bar wasn't across my neck.

11

I tried again, although I knew if I couldn't do it on my first attempt, I was doomed. Call it negative thinking, call it a defeatist attitude, I really don't care. It was me, not you, getting squashed beneath the barbells.

I had several options. First, I could yell for Ellen (who was vacuuming upstairs) and hope she'd hear, but I would feel sheepish asking her for assistance. My pride would suffer. If I was to select this option, I needed to act immediately while enough air remained in my lungs. I decided I'd rather die from suffocation than embarrassment.

Second, I could pray for a shot of adrenaline. I'd heard of one-hundred-pound women lifting cars off persons trapped beneath. "Lord!" I gasped, "as far as I'm concerned, this is a similar emergency." Perhaps I received the surge of hormone, but unfortunately, my muscle power was still too puny.

Third, I could weasel out any way I could. Forget honor and macho; this was survival time. By placing both hands on one end of the bar, I managed to tilt it just enough to slide off the bench to the floor. I lay there for a while, grateful that I had escaped with only a few minor contusions.

One more problem awaited: how to get the bar back to its original position. Steve would find out the truth if I left it diagonally straddling the bench. I had no alternative but to remove the metal discs, set the bar on the rack, and then replace each weight. I made careful note of where each one went so as not to arouse suspicion. Out of curiosity, I totalled the weight on the bar—nearly 200 pounds.

The next day some very sore chest muscles seemed a small price to pay for my indiscretion. However, I did resolve never again to arm wrestle Steve.

Let this story be a lesson to all parents. Raising children is weighty business, a heavy responsibility. To prove it, consider that Ellen and I are exactly the same height—yet some days she towers over me; other times I appear taller than she. The explanation must have to do with which one of us feels more of the weight of the world pressing down. We need extra doses of power often.

The weight-lifting episode caused me to reflect on the nature of strength. Am I a strong father if I have bulky biceps? I suppose so, but only in a superficial way. A truly strong parent is one who is always faithful, always reliable, and always loving. My might is my endurance, my hanging in there. My love for them is a tough love. I don't mean callous or brittle; I mean consistent, persistent and flexible.

I worry sometimes that the concept of tough love, which seems to be in vogue, can be an excuse for plain meanness—lots of "tough," but little "love." Love's toughness, at the core, is always tender, like the father in Luke 15 who didn't lock the door on his wayward son, but opened the door and ran out to greet him.

So eat your heart out, Arnold Schwarzenegger, Franko Columbo, and Lou Ferrigno. I'm stronger than any of you. Go ahead, pump your iron and flex your pectorals. I'll still have my inner strength long after your iron has rusted and your muscles have grown flabby. Three cheers for successful parents! They're the strongest people in the world.

"He delighteth not in the strength of the horse: he taketh not pleasure in the legs of a man. The Lord taketh pleasure in them that fear him, in those that hope in his mercy" (Ps. 147:10, 11).

Two

PUZGETTI

"When I was a child, I spake as a child..." (1 Cor. 13:11). I had particular difficulty saying such words as linoleum and aluminum. I also had a tough time pronouncing my own name, but then so have many articulate adults.

Youngest son David experienced problems with the blended consonants, "sp" being the hardest for him. He could say "spoon" and "sport," but he simply could not master "spaghetti." Over and over again he tried. He carefully formed his lips and tongue correctly. He practiced making an "s" sound until we thought he saw a snake. All to no avail, for out came "puzgetti." Discouragement.

On his sixth birthday, he invited a bunch of young friends to go out for lunch. David wanted to order spaghetti, a dilemma. He grew more and more tense as the waitress moved around the group toward him. "Hi, birthday boy! What would you like to have?"

As David began to stammer and squirm, his cousin Danny mercifully and loudly spoke up. "He wants spaghetti!"

"Yeah, that's what I want." Relief. From that point on he was able to enjoy his party.

Growing up is difficult. There are disappointing experiences to endure, hard lessons to learn, and a number of formidable words to pronounce.

It isn't easy being a parent, either. I heard someone say that the main goal of family life is learning how to stand one another while learning how to love one another. Amen.

I struggled with a non-earthshaking yet irritating problem with my children. I have a difficult time remembering how old each of them is. If they'd remain the same age, I'd do just fine. But when one of them has a birthday, my memory bank flies into turmoil. I'm forced to fall back on my old method—John was born in 1966, of that I'm certain. Steve is seventeen months younger than John and two years older than Amy. Amy was born just before we moved from Nezperce, Idaho, to Bonners Ferry—that was 1970. Therefore, Amy is fourteen. This complicated procedure takes time, but those insurance companies want their forms filled out before they'll pay.

Another puzzlement for this dad is how to determine if they're really and truly sick. Our children seldom fake an illness. But sometimes their symptoms are very vague. "Mom, I don't think I feel good this morning."

"Oh, where don't you feel good?"

"Everywhere."

Our first instinct as parents is to suggest the famous stiff upper lip.

"We know you don't feel well, honey, but you can make it. You'll have to be strong; grin and bear it." A few well-chosen platitudes often succeed. If not, we use firmness.

"You don't have any choice, dear. All of us must fulfill our responsibilities, even when we're sick." With that encouragement, we shove them gently out the door. They can look unbelievably forlorn and abandoned. We feel momentarily guilty for our stern action, but remind ourselves it's for their own good.

Here are some other parental bedside manners which we have effectively employed. After they have announced how sick they are, we put a hand to their forehead while talking about pills large enough to choke elephants and medicine so sour it would make vinegar taste sweet. If this doesn't work, we act delighted that they're sick, and say, "Oh, how wonderful! This means you'll have to stay home. You may start by cleaning your room, dusting the bookshelves, and folding those five piles of clean clothes I didn't get done yesterday. This is my lucky day."

"Uh, Mom, I'm feeling quite a bit better already. Maybe it would be okay if I went to school after all." When they're genuinely ill, they receive our undivided attention and lots of sympathy. If they're only suffering from the "blahs," a bit of imagination can assist in a miraculous recovery.

I am amazed at how many things children are able to learn on their own, yet how many other things we must teach them. There are so many facts and skills to be learned that it requires a team effort. Together with the school's speech expert, we struggled to help David say "spaghetti." He's now got it down perfectly, but it was an uphill struggle. I've helped our children learn how to whistle, ride a bicycle, tie a necktie (which I find impossible to do while facing the youngster), and drive a manual transmission car. But all by themselves they've learned to turn on a television set, track mud, and chew huge wads of bubble gum. I assure you it was without our help that they learned to use the words "awesome" and "totally" ten times in one sentence.

Life brings problems to us that are difficult to surmount, challenges that require every ounce of our energy, and words that are tough to pronouce. The school of hard knocks has no graduation exercises and grants no diplomas. It's a matter of constant learning, of revising inadequate or outdated concepts, of finding a place in old patterns for new ways of doing things.

I get laughed at, or at least smiled at, when I maneuver Michael's bass viol into our small foreign car. The back window has to be rolled down and the bass's neck stuck through it before the door can be shut. It protrudes nearly two feet, so I'm careful not to drive too closely to parked cars and telephone poles. In sub-zero temperatures, it's a chilling experience.

So, David, don't feel bad. At your dad's ripe age, there are still things which don't easily fit, problems I can't solve, and big words that make me tongue-tied. A lot of those tough words jump out at me from the pages of the Old Testament, especially when I'm reading the scripture in church. I just act as though I know what I'm doing.

"Now therefore go, and I will be with thy mouth, and teach thee what thou shalt say" (Ex. 4:12).

Three

THE BEST ME I CAN BE

Stephen got his hair chopped off last spring. Mom was the culprit. She brought out our ancient clippers that once gave me butches and attached the plastic guides. *Buzz buzz.* A pile of dark hair soon lay at her feet. A lot of white scalp showed through, and his ears were prominently visible. The younger children gathered in the kitchen to watch. They were barely able to suppress their laughter. Once in a while, a squeal of amusement escaped. Steve looked in the mirror and proclaimed, "Hey, Mom, looks great!"

"I'm glad you like it, " I quipped, "since it would take a long time to glue it all back on."

Mom subsequently gave crewcuts to a number of Steve's high-school buddies. It seems that short hair is "in" with sixteen-year-old guys. I'm not surprised. Now that we middle-aged males have started growing our hair over our ears and down the back of our necks, what else could our teenagers do to assert their uniqueness? They had to go with flattops to let the world know they could think for themselves. It beats getting a Mohawk.

I imagine when we old-timers start to wear designer jeans, racy tennis shoes, and loud T-shirts, young people will be forced to don three-piece suits, white shirts and ties.

Hey! Maybe I've hit upon a method of improving the appearance of our youth!

If we mature folks look as sloppy as we can, our teens will dress up, if for no reason than to declare their independence.

Our children, including Steve, used to look at our wedding picture and double up in peals of laughter. I didn't perceive this as an expression of compassion. Styles have changed dramatically since 1962 when we were married, but I didn't think I looked that funny. I was just a part of an historical period. But they giggle.

And they ask, "Dad, what did they call *that* hairdo? Fuzztop? Skin head? Prickly pear?" Snicker, snicker. "Do you still have all those lumps and bumps on your head?" More snickers.

I showed remarkable self-discipline after Stephen's haircut. I didn't once remind him of his previous comments about my picture. I even complimented him on his new look. "Your hair will be easy to wash, won't take much shampoo, and the girls will rub your head and say 'Fuzzy Wuzzy was a bear.' " He seemed pleased, though a tad self-conscious. "And your baseball cap will fit perfectly."

Outward styles come and go, and *sometimes* come back again. But I'm the same lovable me inside. I've matured since 1962, and I'm still trying, by the grace of God, to become the best me I can be. I'm one-of-a-kind, an unrepeatable miracle, a limited edition. So is each and every one of God's children.

When I'm being the best me, I'm free from attempting to be like somebody else. I can borrow or copy whatever works, but I'm able to feel good about myself. Therefore I won't try to remake our children after some false image of perfection. I'll let them be the best children or youths they can possibly be.

The best me is sensitive to others, aware of their needs, hopes, and dreams. Over the years I've learned how to "read the signs." When I come home from work, I activate my antennae. Has it been a good day for Mom and the kids? Have they had problems or conflicts? Knowing the lay of the land helps me avoid blunders in greeting them.

When I turn down Brown Street, I fine-tune my powers of observation. Are there any fire trucks, wreckers, or ambulances parked out front? No. Okay, no calamities. Next I check the yard. Bicycles, moped, bat and balls are scattered about. A positive sign.

It means the kids haven't spent much time messing up the inside of the house.

As I pass over the threshold, I listen carefully. Too many loud noises indicate the family's out of control. Too much quiet may mean they're scheming, plotting an ambush.

Then it's my nose's turn. Desirable smells are bread baking, a chocolate cake cooling on the counter, or hair spray and perfume. These indicate that Mom's been able to accomplish something and still found time for herself, even if only a few minutes. I become concerned when the house smells like a hospital room or a steamy gymnasium. The reek of air freshener often gives away an attempt to mask the odor of our burned dinner or of a garbage can that runneth over.

Lastly, I do a visual check. What I hope to see is an average, run-of-the-mill situation. For example, I do not want to see Mom totally wiped out; she'll immediately turn the whole fiasco over to me. On the other extreme, if she is immaculately groomed and looks ravishing, with every hair in place and eye shadow done to perfection, she's probably ready to go out. But I've come to appreciate her in-between, frazzled-gorgeous look. It's the result of her attempt to make the best of two worlds, the adult realm of intelligent conversation and order, and the kids' world of cookie crumbs and dirty sneakers.

The best me is thoughtful and considerate, notices others' thoughtfulness, and is honest, open and available. I recognize that there will always be room for improvement. As someone remarked, that's the biggest room in the house.

"And be not conformed to this world: but be ye transformed by the renewing of your mind, that ye may prove what is that good, and acceptable, and perfect, will of God" (Rom. 12:2).

Four

TIED DOWN AND LIVIN' IT UP

Some days I feel burned out, worked over, buried under, washed up, done in, or otherwise prepositionally exhausted. I'm guessing most parents feel the same way every so often. The fact remains, however, that dads and moms must still hang in, keep on, perk up, get along, go for it. Part of parenting is being tired out from being tied down. It goes with the territory.

I am frequently tied to other people's schedules, both at home and at work: conferences, weddings, counseling sessions, children's piano lessons, Friday night football games, PTA meetings, Cub Scout gatherings, and the like. The list could continue indefinitely. I do have some "release time," but usually it must be snatched between my other commitments. The time frame I can most consistently call "mine" is from 10:00 p.m. until midnight.

I'm not complaining, at least not vehemently, because I've discovered a truth about life. It's good to be tied down, to have people depending on you, to have lots of commitments. It's not good to have it all my own way. I may be tied down, but I'm livin' it up.

It all started with baby John eighteen years ago. I can't recall ever being that tired. It was a hot, muggy New England summer. The upstairs of our old, uninsulated house was stifling by late afternoon. As college students existing barely above the poverty

21

level, we couldn't afford air conditioning. Johnny was breaking out with rash all over his soft little body. Though we tried to entertain him and keep his mind off his misery, he fussed a great deal. It was hard, constant work, requiring loads of energy from us novice parents. What we lacked in skill, we tried to compensate for with effort. I look at him now and wonder how he turned out to be such a fine young man considering the start we gave him. It must have been the grace of God!

We've been tied down ever since. If we have enough time to go somewhere, we don't have enough money. If we have time and money, we probably don't have the energy.

In addition to the children's activities, the pets we've accumulated keep us close to home. It's not easy to find a reliable person willing to feed and exercise two spoiled dogs, one crazy cat, and a neurotic duck. (You'd be neurotic, too, if every visitor made remarks about having you for Thanksgiving dinner—and not as his guest.)

Caring for the house and yard also ties us down. The grass just keeps growing even though I've quit fertilizing it. Fixing three meals a day keeps one from wandering too. If my math is correct, by the time a child completes his eighteenth year at home, somebody will have prepared, served, and cleaned up after 19,710 meals. No wonder fast-food restaurants do a booming business. I wonder how my parents survived without them.

When I came home the other afternoon, I found Ellen up to her pretty elbows in peach juice. Our tree had produced bountifully this year. We tried to give most of the peaches away, but eventually the neighbors said, "No more." So she canned. The jars are beautiful when filled when golden peach halves. But the mess! The kitchen was sticky everywhere—counters, floor, stove, sink. The fruit flies thought they were in heaven. Ellen was tied, or in this case, stuck to her job in more ways than one.

Yes, we're tied down and livin' it up, loving almost every minute. If we weren't tied down, we'd be at loose ends, like an untied shoelace or a kite with no one holding the string. Whatever I've managed to accomplish has been the result of the commitments I've made.

Lo, I tell you a mystery. When you're tied down, only then are you free. When you tie your life to that of Jesus Christ, then do you find peace and joy. When you commit yourself to a spouse, family, and friends, then are you filled with love.

On the one hand, we're stuck with each other. On the other hand, what a fantastic feeling! Because of our security from being bound together, we are set free to be ourselves, free to express our deepest feelings, free to share completely. We have no fear of rejection. We're in this game together, "one for all, and all for one." Our stability provides a foundation on which to create, explore and venture forth. Being tied down permits us to grow and to do what we never could if we were "footloose and fancy free."

We are therefore tied down but not boxed in. Rather than being imprisoned, we are connected to God, to one another, to life and love and power. I praise God for being tied down, linked arm in arm with His people in a way which lifts me up, which encourages and supports me.

Yes, I'm tied down. And I intend to stay in this condition for the remainder of my earthly existence. I believe when that comes to a conclusion, I shall be received into that place not made with hands, and tied together with all the saints of God.

I'm tied down and livin' it up! Amen.

"Delight thyself also in the Lord; and he shall give thee the desires of thine heart. Commit thy way unto the Lord" (Ps. 37:4, 5).

Five

CRIPPLING COMPARISONS

Occasionally, I play the martyr game. The rules are quite simple. I start by grumbling that I work harder than anybody else, get paid less, have the toughest job, and that, if something is to be done right, I have to do it myself. Then, with a pained look, I continue my work feverishly, muttering often. I can't directly ask for any help. If someone were to pitch in, I'd lose because I could no longer complain. It's not a fun game. I never win and I always feel guilty. I should put it back on the shelf to gather dust.

Does it really matter who gets up earlier, works harder, or earns more? Making comparisons is necessary when deciphering how many tablespoons equal a cup, how many cups make a quart, and so forth. The problem comes at the level of comparing persons, their intelligence, athletic abilities, musical talents, and who was given what for Christmas.

"Amy got more than I did. How come?"

"Yeah, I'll bet her presents cost a lot more than mine." The list of possible comparisons is nearly endless.

"How many "A's" did you get on your report card? I got six."

"Look at my mark on the door. I grew an inch more than you did."

"I have naturally curly hair. Don't you wish you did?"

"Our cousins get to stay up later than we do. Uncle Frank and

Aunt Naida are nicer than you. They let Angie watch late-night movies." It seems there is always someone better off than you, and someone else worse off.

Constantly comparing yourself with others can have tragic consequences. Remember the elder brother in Jesus' parable of the prodigal son? (Luke 15).

"Dad," he complained bitterly, "you're playing favorites. I've been a good son. I've always worked hard and obeyed you. But what do I have to show for it? Nothing, except callouses. Then this wild, no-good brother of mine comes crawling home, and you throw a party. I ask you, is that fair to me?"

The elder brother had the blessing of always being with his father, the joy of an unbroken relationship. However, he didn't recognize the blessing because he unfavorably compared his lot to that of his younger brother.

It's a subtle danger. I like to know how I stack up against peers, colleagues, and competitors. So I compare myself. I want our children to perform well, so I measure their accomplishments against those of other youngsters. That might be all right if I didn't take the next step and make my findings public.

"Your cousin Jill made it into advanced orchestra. You could have, too, if you'd tried harder."

"Your older brother made the honor roll all the way through high school. What's wrong with you?"

"When I was your age I paid for all my clothes and entertainment."

The above statements may be true, yet parents must be careful not to use them. They're negative and judgmental. We should expect children to do their best and to work to the limit of their capacity. But we must also make allowances for individual differences and gifts. No two children are alike or equally skilled in any given field. Perhaps Ellen and I are fortunate we have so many offspring that there's at least one who is more intelligent, a better athlete, or a more accomplished musician than we are. And all six are better looking.

Rather than making crippling comparisons, we try to offer healing compliments. We share kind words and stop talking before qualifying or detracting from our praise—"You did a super job, not as good as your sister might have done, but congratulations anyway." We try not to draw too many comparisons in our heads, for neither the "I'm better than" nor the "I'm worse than" variety are helpful. We believe success means fulfilling our God-given potential.

Stephen plays varsity football, though he is relatively small (140 lbs.). He brought home the scouting report for an upcoming game, and the young man he would be facing was exactly one foot taller and one hundred pounds heavier. I expressed concern.

"Don't worry, Dad," he assured. "When we get down in our three-point stance, he'll be the same size I am." By the way, Steve blocked his opponent effectively.

Before school began last fall, we talked to our children about which teachers they might have. David, our youngest, remarked, "I don't want the same teacher John and Mike and Sara had. I want my very own fresh one." He wanted to be accepted as a person in his own right, and not be "so-and-so's brother." I'm certain the teacher would have recognized his individuality; she's a wonderful person. But David didn't want to take any chances.

I shall probably continue making comparisons. I hope, however, to keep my mouth shut and my conclusions to myself. "I'm not as good a preacher as Dr. Lawson. He has a larger vocabulary and a more dramatic presentation. I wonder if the congregation likes me as much as they do him?" Oh, knock it off!

"But the wisdom that is from above is first pure, then peaceable, gentle, and easy to be entreated, full of mercy and good fruits, without partiality, and without hypocrisy" (James 3:17).

Six

HAPPIMESS

I'm sitting in the waiting room of a medical clinic, waiting of course. Steve was blindsided in a football game, suffered temporary memory loss, and is having an electroencephalogram (no wonder they use the acronym EEG). Ellen fell this morning on our sidewalk, gashing her nose and scraping her knees. An earthquake rumbled through the Northwest shortly after 7:00 a.m. and rattled our dishes. One of our cars won't run because battery acid ate through a wire. The roof has a leak that needs to be patched before it rains and I just noticed dark clouds billowing up over the mountains to the west.

Yet I'm joyful. It defies human explanation. It must be a gift of God.

Perhaps I could say my life and our home are filled with "happimess." No, that's not a typo. The "m" is there for good reason. Though our place may be cluttered and ofttimes chaotic, it's also overflowing with love. Hence, the term "happimess."

I won't deny that our children's beds frequently look as though a tag team wrestling match went on all night. From the appearance, it's impossible to determine who won, the kids or the covers.

Sometimes when I shave, I reflect on 1 Corinthians 13:12, "For now we see in a mirror dimly" (RSV) or "through a glass, darkly" (KJV). Paul must have been visiting in a home with children where

27

the mirror was covered with fingerprints, toothpaste splatters, makeup smears. I wonder what teenagers did before the advent of mirrors. Did they gaze into calm waters, squint into polished metal surfaces, or if nothing was available, "go bananas" worrying if every hair was in place? Our car visor is worn out from being repeatedly pulled down to use the mirror on the back.

It's "happimess" all right. Getting ready for church is proof positive. Breakfast is a catch-as-catch-can affair. Bathrooms are clogged with people wiping sleep out of eyes, combing and curling hair, and admiring Sunday dress clothes in the full-length mirror. We're usually on time, barely. But believe me, it's a team effort.

I almost dread returning home afterward. The service needs to be very inspiring and uplifting, knowing the depressing situation awaiting us: clothes strewn all over, cluttered bathrooms, and the kitchen in total disarray. I think the main reason folks go out to eat after Sunday worship is to avoid going home to the catastrophe.

 "Happimess" means there does not have to be outward perfection for inner joy to be present. Our home even has happy dirt. After all, some of it's been around so long it knows it belongs. It's part of the family.

Amy doesn't particularly like shoes. Like her mother, she likes to give her toes freedom to wiggle. Unlike Ellen, however, Amy doesn't feel good with naked feet, so she wears socks everywhere. It may be pouring rain, but Amy seems to think if she runs fast enough they won't get wet. (I wish someone would manufacture white socks with pre-soiled bottoms.) But she's happy and relaxed, so what's a little dirt among friends?

I must mention Steve's room. Toxic fumes seep from underneath his door when he's lifting weights. It's not his fault, just a fact. The humidity is 110% with no sweetness added. It's bad. We should place clothespins outside his door to protect all noses entering his room. If we ever locate the deodorizer that's effective in his room, an advertising agency can use us for a testimonial.

"Happimess" is a regular occurrence in nearly every family's life. Steve went out on one of his first big dates recently, the Homecoming extravaganza and dinner for two at an elegant restaurant. He wore a classy, gray tweed sports coat with patches on the elbows. I've been coveting a coat like that for years. An author *ought* to wear one. I don't want to smoke a pipe. I really don't desire a racy sports car. All I want is a coat with patches on the sleeves. So who gets one? Not Dad.

In making himself charming, Steve left the bathroom and his bedroom in shambles. We decided not to clean up after him, figuring it was his job to do the next day. The next day arrived on schedule; Steve's resolve to pick up did not. I grew impatient, and although I knew it to be poor parenting technique, I started cleaning. I entered his room and found his brand new tweed coat in a heap on the floor! Lucky for him it doesn't quite fit me, or he'd be minus one tweed coat with elbow patches.

He did enjoy a wonderful night on the town. And we were proud as our handsome young man left arm in arm with a cute girl friend. It was one more illustration of what I'm talking about: "happimess."

Maybe this is how it has always been and will forever be. Perhaps what counts in this business of parenting isn't a neatly packaged product, but rather the process of loving, working and struggling together. Who cares if everything goes perfectly, all tidy and neat, with no surprises or interruptions? The significant thing is that we live in harmony and thankfulness, and are on the way to becoming the individuals and family that God wants us to be. If the choice is between (1) neat but grouchy, and (2) grimy but joyful, I'll take the latter every time. Let's celebrate "happimess"!

"Behold, we count them happy which endure. Ye have heard of the patience of Job. . ." (James 5:11).

Seven

LOOKING UP IN A WORLD THAT LOOKS DOWN

Michael floundered through a mildly awkward stage in his growth. It was nothing dramatic, but enough to cause a rash of accidents, including three collarbone fractures. One time he ground off several large patches of skin by flying over his bicycle handlebars and skidding across the asphalt.

After he had healed, I suggested he pay more attention to where he was going. "I try," he shrugged, "but somehow I get there faster than I expect."

"Michael, it's like playing catch. Keep your eye on the ball and don't look down at your hands or the mitt. They'll do what they're supposed to if you watch the ball." He gave me a blank look.

"I thought we were talking about bicycles."

"We are, son. Sorry for the detour. What I mean is, look up and ahead of you. Don't concentrate on where you've been, but learn to watch where you're heading."

"I get it. I must have steered crooked when I looked back to see how far ahead of David I was."

"Precisely."

Looking up and forward is a difficult lesson to learn since we live in a world that usually looks down, or backwards, or sideways. It seldom looks up to view the glory of its Creator. It rarely looks to the future to glimpse the wonderful gifts God wants to give us.

I think we parents often train our children to look too low. "Tie your shoelaces before you trip on them." "Look at the mess you've made on the floor." "Watch your step." Loose shoelaces may be a nuisance; messy floors may be unpleasant. But inability to see God's handiwork in nature or to respond to smiling faces is a tragedy.

I want our children to be "up" lookers, to have confidence in themselves, to make eye contact with people, to see the beauty of the earth. I want them to go through life not downcast, but able to face each new day with a hope-filled countenance.

I need people to whom I can look up to, giants of the faith whose accomplishments inspire and challenge me. Frankly, there are too few persons today worthy of looking up to as models and heroes. A rock star with limited musical ability and a questionable lifestyle hardly qualifies. Nor do sports figures who seem more interested in mega-salaries, no-cut contracts, and "superstar" images. We should not pick on the rich and famous exclusively, however. Teachers, preachers, law-enforcement personnel, or business leaders can become so concerned about their success and advancement that they fail to be solid examples for others. Our young people need adults of integrity after whom they can pattern their lives.

The problem of disrespectful youth stems partially from a world which has not proved itself deserving of their respect. Community and national leaders, the media, major institutions, and even parents have not always earned the admiration of young persons.

There is entirely too much looking down these days. An ethnic group looks down on others. A Christian denomination looks askance at churches whose doctrines vary even slightly from its own. A socio-economic class looks down its nose at a so-called lower class. Adults look down on youth and say, "They're going to the dogs." Youth look down on adults, claiming, "They don't know where it's at."

It's about time for some upward, forward looking. There is majesty and beauty all around us. There are people who need our support and guidance and who are eager to share theirs with us. There is a future with splendid possibilities.

I have serious concerns about what the shape of the future will be. What kind of society will our children inherit from us? Will it be in such turmoil or so corrupt as to offer little hope? They deserve a secure and stable world in which to dream and plan and build. Perhaps it's a selfish desire, but I want to be able to sit in a rocking chair in my older years and cuddle my grandchildren.

It may come to pass. If one person stands on a street corner gazing up, a crowd will soon do likewise, though they won't have the foggiest notion what they're supposed to be seeing. So, in the hope that someone else may join me, I'm going to keep looking up. And if I'm asked at what or to whom I'm looking, I'll be ready with the answer.

"I will lift up mine eyes unto the hills, from whence cometh my help. My help cometh from the Lord, which made heaven and earth" (Ps. 121:1).

Eight

THE DIARY OF A GLAD DAD

It had a catchy title: *The Diary of a Mad Housewife.* I don't recall the theme of the book and its resultant movie, but I can create an imaginary scenario.

The walls of the house closed ever tighter. Noises echoed from wall to wall, chasing her through the house. Everything needed cleaning. Kids were swinging from the light fixtures. Snap! She went "bananas," her personality now matching her split-level home.

I wish to offer an opposite and happy story—the diary of a glad dad. The following are entries from my journal telling of good experiences, moments of unity and wholeness.

October 27
Fall is in full flavor. The setting sun spreads a red blush across the sky.

Saturday night the high school youth group had a spaghetti feed at church, and I promised to be a wandering violinist. I wish I hadn't. I'm exhausted from ministerial duties. I tried to practice and couldn't hit one note, let alone play a whole song. Discouragement! I dutifully brought my fiddle to the affair—and hid it in my office. Somebody remembered my promise, so I gave it my best shot. And *voilà*, we made music. With guitar and piano accompaniment, it sounded great. I was no longer weary. In fact, they couldn't get me to quit. Maybe this is a parable for the family. When I attempt to be a "Lone Ranger" parent, I become easily discouraged. When we work and play together, we inspire one another and have a delightful time.

The south wall of our house is weathering. The paint is cracking and a few nails are pulling loose. I put two coats of expensive paint on it just a few years ago. It shouldn't be doing that. But of course it's weathering; it's exposed to the blistering August sun and the drenching rains in spring. It's right out there being soaked and bleached. Let me also praise God for the signs of my personality weathering: the touch of gray at the temples, wrinkles indented more deeply around my eyes and mouth, the sore muscles and joints following hard physical exercise. It means (like the wall) I've been open, accessible, and vulnerable.

October 30

It's good to be a father. I'm tired, got no money, and I'm short on answers. But, Lord, I'm full of joy anyway! Amen.

We rearranged Sara's bedroom. I grump about such procedures, though I really don't mind. With winter rapidly gaining on us, it will give her more floor space for indoor play.

Lord, thank you for expecting me to reorder my life from time to time. When furniture stays in one place, dust balls form and cobwebs attach. Change brings a chance to houseclean, to freshen up. Move me, Lord, so I don't grow stale and moldy.

November 3

It's Michael's tenth birthday. Makes *me* feel older as well. To where did chubby little Michael disappear? And who is this lanky boy standing before me? He had sixteen friends at his party. I planned a treasure hunt at the park. My, how those skinny kids can run! I ate too much, ran too hard, laughed a lot, and am now exhausted. Ain't life grand? It's a good thing birthdays happen only once a year.

June 29

The rain came down in torrents. Gushing streams cascaded

down gutters and backed up storm drains. The neighborhood children took off their shoes and socks, rolled up their pant legs, and cavorted in the water. Now that's what I call "Showers of Blessing!"

July 6

I survived the Fourth of July—barely. I cautioned the kids and cousins to be careful with sparklers, ground flowers, and lady fingers. Then I shot off a massive shower of sparks which promptly tipped over and sent fireballs whizzing into adjacent yards and at everybody's legs. I never saw folks move so fast while screaming and yelling. Such a celebration! I wonder what I can do to top that spectacle next year.

July 20

Our twentieth anniversary. Amy and Sara served us breakfast in bed—orange juice, toast strips, a donut, and raspberries with whipped cream. It was excellent! Sara had to make three or four trips up the stairs to encourage us to stay in bed, once following a loud crash in the kitchen. "It'll be okay. We dropped something. But don't worry, we're cleaning it up."

January 5

What a concert we're having tonight—a special treat of after-dinner entertainment. Mike is sawing away on his bass viol while Sara plucks her cello (two different songs, naturally); John has his TV blaring; Amy is lifting leg weights in time to loud music; somebody is pounding on the piano; and the dishwasher is swishing away. Steve, at least, is using earphones so the music from his tape deck doesn't bother me, but I wish he'd quit tapping his feet and drumming his fingers. Enjoy it, Dad. You're blessed with an active, happy family.

February 27

Four of our children took part (actually, the word is "starred") in a church school musical production. Mike was Pharaoh, Sara did a cute frog dance, and Amy sang in a trio. David, who was so shy last year he hid behind brother Mike, stood right in front and belted out his part. What a difference a year makes! When the group did the concluding number, he stole the show. It was hilarious because he was totally unself-conscious.

May 24

May is a busy month. Ellen had two meetings to attend this evening—a church women's circle and PTSA board meeting. I was supposed to grace three meetings with my presence. We compromised and played hooky from them all, then took the children to the high school orchestra's spring concert. It was a deliciously irresponsible decision, and we all enjoyed it.

"Therefore my heart is glad, and my glory rejoiceth: my flesh also shall rest in hope" (Ps. 17:9).

Nine

WITH SIGHS TOO DEEP FOR WORDS

In the eighth chapter of Romans, Paul wrote that the Spirit helps us in our weakness "with groanings which cannot be uttered" (v. 6). A modern version uses the phrase, "with sighs too deep for words." That's a good description of parenting, at least on some days. Show me a parent who takes his or her job seriously, and I'll show you an experienced groaner and sigher.

Stephen elected to stay home one lazy Sunday afternoon while the rest of the family went to a street fair. We were gone for perhaps two hours. During that time, Steve, growing boy that he is, ate several pieces of cake which were being saved for dessert, wolfed down four slices of toast spread with inch-thick jelly, finished the Spaghettios left from lunch, polished off a box of cereal, guzzled the rest of the orange juice, and topped it off with a heaping bowl of ice cream and a handful or two of chocolate chip cookies. Mom had instructed him to clean his room while we were gone. Obviously, he hadn't had an opportunity. He was too busy eating. We could have gotten justifiably upset, but what was the use? We just breathed in deeply, and as a duet, sighed together.

Sighing is a required skill for parents. When words won't suffice, when verbal expression cannot capture the height of joy nor the valley of disappointment, a sigh is the perfect vehicle. Perhaps it's a way of relaxing, of preparing to receive an influx of God's power. I think of sighs as unspoken prayers.

There are occasions when we're up all night with a sick child (sigh), or when a youth is caught in the swirl of a bad mood and can't seem to recover (sigh). David ate red berries from a bush because he thought they were a new kind of raisin. After we rushed him to the emergency room and had his stomach pumped, he was fine. We collapsed (sigh). At 10:30 p.m. Steve remembered his football jersey had to be laundered by tomorrow morning (sigh). And what about the times there's been no bread for breakfast or school lunches, and it's *midnight* (sigh). Add the losses, failures, and sorrows, and sighing becomes crucial.

I fear sighing is a vanishing art. I therefore recommend regular practice, including the formation of parent groups designed to teach and encourage sighing. Too many persons are unskilled in this field. For example, few know the basic types of sighing and their stages of progression.

First is the shoulder-shrug sigh. It usually expresses attitudes such as, "How should I know?" or "Who cares?" or "You're going to do what you want anyway." I frequently accompany it with up-turned hands and a nervous chuckle.

Second is the familiar catch-my-breath-sigh. In the midst of a hectic day, when my body is low on energy but there's barely a dent made in the list of duties, this type of sigh can do wonders. I inhale deeply and then quickly exhale, making a "whew" sound through an open mouth. It helps if someone is near enough to hear. It advertises what a hard-working, diligent person I really am. Done correctly, it can accomplish more than any amount of complaining.

Third is the oh, my, sigh: "Oh, my, is this happening to me?" or "Oh, my, what else could possibly go wrong?" It works best if I place several fingers alongside the forehead and slightly furrow my brow. It is appropriate after experiencing that one thing too many: a juice-spill on the rug, a clogged sink, an ungrateful family at dinner, or an argument over which television show to watch— "You always get to watch what you want, and I never do. It's not fair!"

"Dad, Steve's changing the channel! I was watching *Diff'rent*

Strokes. You told me I could." I can't remember whether I did or didn't. Just in case, I order Steve to keep his hands off the channel selector.

"But, Dad, there's a great special on channel five. My civics teacher told us to watch it." I search for the television guide to see what the special is, check the clock to see how much longer *Diff'rent Strokes* will last, and do an oh, my, sigh (this is the perfect sigh to employ when I can't win no matter how hard I try). Someone is certain to glare at me accusingly and demand that justice be done. There is no way I can satisfy everybody.

Fourth is the release-the-pressure sigh. It is proper to utter the famous "arrrrgh" at the same time. I had barely finished chewing out a child when I discovered I'd goofed. Not only had I overreacted to a very minor problem, but somebody else was the culprit. I felt guilty, wished I could undo my actions and take back my sharp words. Since I could not, I clenched my teeth, frowned and mumbled, "Why did I do that? What a dummy I am." I sighed. It didn't change anything other than calm my inner turmoil.

Fifth is the totally-done-in sigh, made by slumping on the sofa or easy chair, lowering the head to the chest, and slowly expelling air with a quiet "oh-h-h." It is often heard at the end of a long day. The work may not be done (is it ever?), but I simply cannot keep going (sigh). I find it sometimes helpful to use this sigh prior to going to bed, as it relaxes my whole body. A wide yawn ideally complements this sigh.

The sixth, and the ultimate, is the turn-it-over-to-the-Lord sigh. When all else has failed; when every road leads to a dead end; when no answer is adequate, it's time to sigh, "Oh, Lord." This is short for, "Oh, Lord, I've tried. I've done everything I could think of. You've just got to help." This sigh does quite nicely in place of an "Amen."

Whistling is a good device to pick up a flagging spirit. Singing likewise can lift the soul. But the ability to sigh is absolutely essential for parents and for others who are struggling to make it through the day.

Are you ready? Inhale; 1—2—3; exhale and sigh. Repeat as necessary.

"For my sighs are many, and my heart is faint" (Lam. 1:22).

Ten

QUIET THOUGHTS IN A LOUD WORLD

I looked up *noise* in my trusty thesaurus—"loud, clangorous, bedlam, hubbub, tumult, earsplitting, rambunctious, piercing." Roget must have been writing under circumstances similar to mine. At this moment three of our youngsters are sprawled on the living room carpet playing Candy Land. Mike is laughing boisterously at Sara, who is squawking loudly. David is cheering them both on. Even with my door shut and the radio going, the clamor filters in.

Human ears have been forced to deal with noise from the beginning of time, but increased population, industrialization, and electronic inventions have made noise far more prevalent today. We can take noise with us everywhere; or, depending on our perspective, we can't get away from it anywhere. With communications satellites encircling the globe, we can name our noise and carry it from city street to wilderness trail. One minor problem: I don't want to have it everywhere.

I recently went hunting for some quiet and found it to be an elusive prey. As I sat at the picnic table in our backyard, a sudden breeze rustled through the treetops. The wind chimes Grandpa made bumped lyrically together. Birds chattered in nearby bushes, sometimes scolding one another, sometimes joyfully praising their Creator. Flies buzzed hither and yon in the warm September air.

A dry leaf skittered across the cement patio. A constant low rumble came from a distant highway. Somewhere down the street a youth practiced his trumpet. A neighbor mowed his lawn. Several blocks away a hammer whacked methodically.

I realized then that even in the middle of the night, total quiet is an impossibility. Ambulance and police sirens announce new emergencies in the community. Crashes from the rail yard indicate a switch engine is busily at work. It's up to me to select what I shall, and shall not, hear.

I remained at the picnic table, and a butterfly flitted silently by. Or did it? I wondered, is its flight actually soundless, or are my ears just too dull to hear the movement of its graceful wings?

God's still, small voice is speaking to people in these days. We cannot hear it in the earthquakes of nations fighting nations, or in the mighty winds of crass materialism. There are too few quiet moments in the hectic lives of most families. Oh, we pause briefly before meals to return thanks. And there are sporadic family devotions. I confess, though I am a pastor, devotions do not come easily. Perhaps I have never quite recovered from my rebellious younger days when family worship was pleasantly enforced. I had to read from a small booklet that seldom related to anything I was doing.

For our family, I find most helpful what might be called "serendipitous devotions." I can't plan these in advance, but I can be ready when they happen. God will provide the raw materials, often in surprising ways and in unexpected places.

One magic moment of calm comes when children are in bed but haven't yet drifted off to sleep. They're motionless and in an excellent position to listen—prone. During daylight hours, the only way to slow them down is to tackle and sit on them. An unhurried bedtime is filled with precious possibilities. We squeeze further happiness from the day's joys. We talk about anxieties that tomorrow may bring. We often touch—hugs and kisses, and speak to God through prayer.

One evening Ellen and I trudged wearily down the stairs to tell Michael and David good night. They were snuggled in their bunk beds, reading their Bibles. David's was brand new, given to him by the church when he entered third grade. His look was a mixture of pride and confusion.

"What are you reading, Dave?" I inquired.

"Something called Le-vit-i, um-m-m, I can't pronounce it." He held his Bible open for me to look. He had been struggling to understand burnt offerings and oblations.

"David, Leviticus is a great book, but I think you might like Psalms better, or maybe one of the Gospels." We turned to Psalm 100.

His eyes lit up as he read, "Make a joyful noise unto the Lord, all ye lands" (v. 1).

Another time when God's still, small voice can be heard is while traveling. As we drive down the road, we're in close quarters with no possible escape. In our crowded station wagon, we have two options: pick at each other, or enjoy each other's company. We can spend the duration arguing and disagreeing; or we can play games, sing happy songs, relax, and even worship.

Outdoor activities are alive with possibilities for closeness to God and to each other. Sitting quietly beside a gurgling brook and holding hands around a crackling campfire as dusk creeps down the mountainside are profound experiences. Our most recent acquired family pastime has been cross-country skiing. As we silently glide among fir trees and over meadows white with virgin snow, we gain both needed exercise and inner peace. I even praise God for cold noses and "toeses."

"Be still, and know that I am God..." (Ps. 46:10a).

Eleven

HOW TO UNTIE STOMACH KNOTS

As a Boy Scout I learned how to tie and untie square knots, bowlines, and sheepshanks. I already knew how to do a granny knot. But I received no instructions or merit badges for untying knots that form in the pit of the stomach. And believe me, those can be just as tight and complicated as rope knots.

Let me illustrate. Sara literally dragged herself home from school. She had no specific complaints; she just didn't feel well. She picked at the food on her dinner plate, though it was something she usually relished. Normally a quiet girl, she yelled at her brothers so loudly I feared our glass chandelier might shatter. One comfort: her dillydallying before bed was a common practice. But the accumulation of strange behavior began to make us wonder. Sara finally crawled into bed, then immediately jumped up for a drink of water. Back under the covers again, she suddenly remembered something she'd left in the bathroom. Her bed could have been a trampoline for all the bouncing she was doing.

In a rare moment of calm, I tiptoed in and lay on the floor next to her bed. We held hands. Before long the story began tumbling out of her ten-year-old head.

She talked about pressures she was feeling at school—not from the academic work but from friends who were competing for her attention—"Play with me at recess. If you play with so-and-

46

so, I won't like you anymore." Sara was so knotted up inside she was unable to relax. After an hour's discussion, her eyelids slowly closed and she slept.

Some stomach knots slip apart quickly and easily. At other times, their tangled mess requires much patience just to undo a few strands. I was taught the lesson of going slowly when I helped comb the hair of one of our little girls. After a number of anguished "Yeows!" I stopped trying to untangle it all with one or two swipes of the comb.

We parents need to know which knots they're dealing with to determine how best to untie them. We must be able to distinguish between minor upsets and major catastrophes. It's a discernment I have not yet mastered. Fortunately, Ellen has, so we complement each other very nicely in this matter. My response to any and all crises is to panic, run around excitedly, and assume the worst has happened. I'd make a terrible emergency room nurse. Ellen's style, on the other hand, is outward calm. She coolly examines the injury or damage and rationally decides the appropriate course of action: whether to kiss the "ouchy," apply a Band-Aid, consult our family physician, or head to the hospital. But as soon as the decision's been made, she falls apart and starts shaking like a leaf. By then, I've managed to quit blubbering and have sufficiently reorganized my act to assume responsibility. It's an effective system. Together we're a capable team for comforting hurts, bringing healing to most upsets, and untying even the worst stomach knots.

I have difficulty finding ways to untie the knots in my own midsection. Since I have a larger middle than my children do, the knots can be bigger with more kinks and twists. It would be grand if I could prevent these knots from ever forming. Realistically, there are too many forces effective at tying me up.

I cope better when I'm well-rested, but adequate sleep and relaxation are not always possible. Therefore I need to be as patient with myself as I try to be with others. I'm human and can tangle things up without trying. While I do become unnecessarily alarmed on occasion, I do not need to invite in the big, bad wolf of panic, no matter how much he huffs, puffs, or bluffs. I shall try to whistle a happy tune while I parent, and pray for God's calming influence.

I am attempting to stop getting tied up inside by minor irritations, such as sunflower seeds scattered on the floor. Maybe our wastebaskets can't catch what's thrown their way. Some days the baskets seem to miss more than they catch.

I'm knotted up right now. Not badly, just a small tangle or two. One of our cars coughed and died this evening. I must decide if it can be fixed or if a funeral must be planned. Steve received a concussion playing football last week but wants to play in this Friday's game. Mom, Dad and the doctor don't agree with him, and the tension is producing that churning feeling beneath my navel. I'm struggling to lose a couple of pounds before Thanksgiving, but I've got three potlucks and one progressive dinner to attend—and somebody brought Almond Roca to the office today.

Lord, I could use a pep talk. Wipe my fevered brow. Restore my trust in you. Fill my soul with peace and power.

"And into whatsoever house ye enter, first say, Peace be to this house" (Luke 10:5).

Twelve

OH, THE HAPPIER WE GET TOGETHER

On the wall of our bedroom is a portrait of Ellen's great grand-mother, and one of her grandfather and his brother. The frames are ornate and the poses somber. Apparently, when photographs were made in the last century, smiles were out and steely eyes with tight lips were "in." I'm certain they had many happy times and lots of laughter, but the pictures don't even hint at it. Pictures of our family today are quite a contrast: cheesy grins and ham-ming it up fill the frames.

We enjoy each other's company, but the old song, "The More We Get Together, the Happier We Will Be," is not accurate. Mere togetherness is no guarantee of happy experiences. In fact, close proximity often produces friction and conflict. However, it is very true that the more happy times we have as a family, the stronger we become. It might be more precise to say (or sing if you wish), "The Happier We Get Together, the More We Will Be."

Ellen and I were relaxing/collapsing at the end of a hectic day. Seven-year-old David wandered into the living room, climbed up on Ellen's lap, snuggled against her shoulder, and sighed, "Ah, luxury." He was precisely right. Cuddling produces special feelings of comfort, security and love. I have days when I could use some lap time, someone to assure me "all's well with the world," or at least with my small corner of it.

Ellen recently completed weeks of sorting and organizing family photographs. Several years' photos had accumulated. It's easy to get behind on such duties. They're not pressing demands such as cooking or laundering. She bought fifteen albums and began her arduous task. When the last picture had been slipped into place, we had the grand unveiling. What joy! Our children each grabbed a book and sprawled on the front room carpet. Squeals of delight punctuated the evening as they remembered the past and observed how much they had grown. It took several days for them to peruse the entire collection, especially since they had to pause frequently to joke about the most hilarious shots.

I have come to realize we cannot program the truly meaningful and significant moments in our family. We can provide opportunities, but we cannot by our efforts alone produce the deepest joys. I cannot say, "All right, children, I've got an hour for you to relate to me on a meaningful level. Let's get with it." Parents must be flexible to respond to spontaneous events, to be moved when imaginations are sparking and hearts are melting.

Of course, there are special days in which we work harder to create the right atmosphere for happiness: birthdays, holidays, vacation outings. A "happiness" event for our family is our annual trek to the Apple Blossom Parade. We lug popcorn, peanut butter sandwiches, and picnic benches to the home of our friends, Anne and Brev. They live on the parade route, so we stake our claim to their curb space. We munch on our goodies and watch band after band prance by. There are impossible traffic jams and a crush of excited people, but it's a thrilling time for us.

In the same season, we observe another enjoyable custom: giving May baskets. I fear it's a vanishing tradition. Not many people today create these delicate arrangements of tiny violets, dandelions, rosebuds, or whatever's available. We have fun watching our children use their imaginations with construction paper, to add cheery words of greeting. Then they run through the neighborhood depositing their gifts on the doorsteps of unsuspecting friends. May Day is one of the few unspoiled holidays left. When else is giving done for the pure joy of it, expecting nothing in return? I'm all for the revival of May Day, but not by commercial-izers.

Our family has had some great laughs. Often, around the dinner table, one of us says something that may (or may not) intentionally be funny. The laughing is infectious and once we get started, it's difficult to bring to a halt. But then, why should we want to stop laughter? There's far too little of it in this weary world. It's important that we laugh with one another. If we have the ca-pacity to laugh *with* each other, we will laugh less *at* each other. Humor has the potential to defuse otherwise tense moments, and to turn an argument into a positive discussion.

Along with laughter, let's increase the amount of "heart lan-guage" in the home. I want to be a love-and-touch dad who shares inner feelings and is available. I'm not a remote control device, but a caring and tender person. I want to be open to feel their joys, even if it makes me vulnerable to their hurts. The payoff is so precious, it's worth the risk, and then some.

"For the Holy Spirit, God's gift, does not want you to be afraid of people, but to be wise and strong, and to love them and enjoy being with them" (2 Tim. 1:7, TLB).

Thirteen

A POOR LOSER BUT A GOOD SPORT

I do not like losing. I'm familiar with the old sports adage, "Show me someone who likes to lose and I'll show you a loser." Well, whether it pleases me or not, I often come out second best. Being left-handed helps me win at Ping-Pong, until my opponent makes the neccessary adaptations. I can still throw my weight around enough to come out ahead playing basketball with my sons and daughters. I'm pretty sharp at checkers, but I can never win at chess.

Reality is closing in on me. My reflexes are slowing down. My eyes are dimming. Gravity has tugged on my muscles for so many years that they've sagged toward the middle. It's progressive and apparently irreversible. I have to compensate by using my experience and brain power. That works for card games, but is far less effective when running hundred-yard dashes. The mind may improve with age. Legs assuredly do not.

While it may be difficult to cope with losing, I'm discovering it's good for me, a valuable lesson in humility. And it's a good experience for my children to beat me. My authority as a parent is not based on always winning. I may get boxed in by Michael's king when playing checkers and financially ruined in Monopoly by landing on John's Boardwalk (with hotel). Those are the risks of the game.

I'm human and vulnerable. The dice don't roll any better for me because I'm their father. I'm tempted to play only those games I'm sure of winning. But where's your courage, old man? Come on, accept the challenge and risk it.

I try to be a good sport when I lose. It sounds rather classy to say, "I'm being philosophical in the face of defeat." Anyway, I would rather teach my children to lose graciously than to win at any cost. I want all of us to be fair and just, not only in games but in every endeavor.

It's important to play by the rules. Frequently one of us, sometimes Dad, tries to make up new rules in the heat of the contest. "Whaddya mean the sidewalk's out-of-bounds? I say it's the bushes. So I was in-bounds and we win!" I've observed that rule changes seldom work to the disadvantage of their inventor. If nice guys and gals finish last in basketball and football, so be it. Kindness finishes first in the final standings, and that's according to the Official Scorebook.

The graceful way is simply to admit defeat, smile sweetly, congratulate the winner, and not become uptight. Thank the Lord, my sports prowess does not determine my self-image. Were that the case, I'd be in a heap of trouble.

When the team I'm rooting for loses, I experience a letdown. But I'm faithful and stick by them. I've been a Seattle Seahawks fan since their inception. There hasn't been a whole lot to cheer about through the years, yet it's been satisfying. I identify with the players and coaches, and I pull for them all the harder when they're underdogs—which is most of the time.

I've had mostly positive experiences with the world of sports. I appear rather comical on roller skates and inept at billiards, and I do a good imitation of a rock in the swimming pool, but I have a good time trying. Playing together as a family permits the release of tension and serves as an outlet for aggression. A little bumping and pushing in an active game may do wonders for relationships. So much of our lives is verbal or passive. It's wonderful to cross-country ski through the orchard across the street, build snow forts and peg snowballs at each other (except when baseball pitcher Steve plastered Dad in the eye). It's relaxing to bicycle through back streets in town or throw a Nerf football in the front yard. And it's all a lot healthier than plopping in front of the TV set.

I will probably never find it easy to lose. I can even become perturbed losing at solitaire. But I'm trying to be a good sport about it. I'm attempting to live according to the example of Paul who wrote, "I have learned, in whatsoever state I am, therewith to be content" (Phil. 4:11). I want to be content both in life's victories and defeats.

Maybe I am not so much a bad loser as a bad winner. Whatever the outcome, though, I really do wish to be a good sport, showing more concern for my friends and family than for the final score. I play for enjoyment and not for a fabulous individual performance.

I make no apologies for playing aggressively. My goal is to never humiliate another person, and I hope he returns the favor. I believe the best games are those in which everyone participates and all come out winners.

I shall never be a world-class athlete in any pursuit. It simply isn't in the cards—or in the muscles, coordination or timing. But I can be a world-class good sport. Anyone for tiddlywinks?

"The race is not to the swift, nor the battle to the strong" (Eccles. 9:11).

Fourteen

FIVE TO NINE IS TWICE AS LONG

Bless her heart. Ellen had calculated and charted everything that had to be done from the time school got out until bedtime; she had written "Ellen" or "Kel" beside each of our appointed tasks. I got scared just looking at the list. Even Ellen, whose mind is hard to boggle, was apprehensive.

The string instruments had to be carted home from the school music room. Mike needed encouragement to do his paper route. Sara needed a ride to her piano lesson. Steve would have to be picked up after football practice. I had two important church meetings and a counseling session. There was an informational meeting for parents of sixth graders regarding an upcoming school camp, followed by open house during which we would have to visit three rooms, carefully spending equal amounts of time in each. Ellen had a PTA board meeing sandwiched in between. John was at his job and would need a ride home. Amy had to be taken to junior high drill team practice and David to a Cub Scout den meeting. And we would need to bring them home from different directions and at different times. Somewhere in this flurry of activity, dinner was to be cooked and eaten, the pets fed, and Mom and Dad were expected to make themselves presentable for their public appearances.

We made it. Shortly after we arrived home for the last time

that night, the telephone rang. I had just slipped on my comfy bathrobe, plunked down in front the late news, and was contemplating fixing a snack. The snack never materialized. In response to a family's crisis, I was out till 3:00 a.m.

The hours spent at a job, devoted to work outside the home, are demanding, significant, and require considerable energy. Like the three secretaries in the movie *Nine to Five*, we struggle to endure the hassle, master the skills, get along with other workers, and deal with customers.

But no matter how long those hours may seem, nine to five is only half as long as five to nine. These sixteen hours must also be planned and wisely used. Like the eight (or more) hours at work, the rest of each day is filled with pitfalls and opportunities.

Five to nine is not simply twice as long, it's also twice as difficult to organize. It's untidy and unpredictable, hectic one day, unruffled the next, a mixture of chaos and calm. There's no time clock to punch. It's up to us to manage these hours. When confusion is in charge around the house, I escape to the office to soothe my soul. On other occasions, I crawl home seeking solace and TLC after a tough day at work. Woe is me when neither place offers peace. When home and office are both in turmoil, my ultimate goal is survival.

There are certainly stresses and strains in family life. Right now, noise is the one with which I'm trying to cope. Two radios are having a duel (I wish one would win); Amy is tooting her flute; and somebody is "baby talking" to the dogs. I can't stand that gibberish. No baby I've ever known talked like that. In addition, Sara's practicing for a recital. She's playing Beethoven's "Russian Folk Song" for the two hundredth time, and that's a conservative estimate. Thank goodness it's quality music. Still, I'd welcome a little variety.

There are also time binds. I can't do everything at once; I must prioritize my various duties and opportunities. Is a spotless kitchen equal in value to holding a child on my lap? Is a neatly trimmed lawn more important than playing tag on shaggy grass?

People often ask me where I get the time to write. I don't get the time. I make it, create it. I squeeze it from moments that otherwise might be wasted, or at least not used productively. I love to write, so I find ways to do it.

How are we going to spend those hours away from the office, the store, the assembly line? I suppose we can sit transfixed in front of our television sets while our brains turn to jello. But why not use the time wisely: to build family relationships; to help out as a thoughtful spouse; to study and pray and worship; to pursue hobbies; to play and relax.

We Americans need lessons in relaxing. We seem to bring the same tension to our "play" as we do to our work. We turn everything into contests to see who's the strongest, fastest, smartest. We think we can't have fun unless we spend bundles of money on recreational equipment. Uptight at work or at home or at play, what's the difference? The cost is high, even though we get paid for the one.

I attempt not to play the job against my family-times, and vice versa. I don't want to bring problems and anxieties home and "dump truck" them on Ellen and the kids. I do it sometimes, but I have a few therapeutic mental exercises I do as I drive home. I sing a happy song, talk pleasantly to myself (who cares what people in oncoming vehicles think?). I prepare to reenter home life, readying myself to listen, to pitch in where I'm needed. It is seldom possible for me to collapse when I arrive home. So I tell myself I'll have a chance to do so later. At first, there are stories to be shared about school, about field trips to the county fair, about blue stars and smile faces on papers, about homework problems, about what's for dinner (and "Do I have to eat it?") and, and . . .

I want our family to fill the hours available to us with experiences which draw us closer to each other and expand our knowledge and our joy. We need times of relaxation and laughter, serious moments and deep discussions, times of intense concentration and others of doing absolutely nothing.

We spend approximately half of the span from 5 p.m. to 9 a.m. asleep. Ellen and I seldom get it all at once, uninterrupted or unedited. However, I don't want us to doze our family life away. We are called by God to live abundantly, with vigor.

Somebody ought to film a sequel of *Nine to Five* called *Five to Nine*. I could supply a lot of material for the script.

"So teach us to number our days, that we may apply our hearts unto wisdom" (Ps. 90:12).

Fifteen

DADS GET LONELY, TOO

I'm on my way to San Francisco for six weeks, back to school after fifteen years away. I hope I can survive it. The academic work concerns me less than the separation from my family. I've often been gone several days at a stretch—but forty-two days? And in the summer when we usually spend extra time together? I'm not confident of how well I'll cope.

It was a long first day on the road as I felt frequent twinges of loneliness. I controlled it (almost) by keeping up constant chatter with Norm, my traveling companion. As I unpacked at our motel in Redding, I unearthed a family photo in my suitcase. I felt a mixture of pride and pain. I had planned to wait till later in the evening to call home, but I couldn't. I had to do it immediately.

It's depressing to think of all I'll miss, including Steve's and Amy's August birthdays. Perhaps I'd better not look ahead quite so far. I'll try to concentrate on the stimulating ideas I'm about to learn and the wonderful people I'll meet.

Goodness, if I missed them that much on the first day, what would it be like in three weeks? I might be a basket case. However, feeling lonely is a positive sign. It shows I love them, that our relationships are deep. We can make it for six weeks!

I arrived safely in San Anselmo, a charming community nestled in the rolling hills and eucalyptus trees across the Golden

Gate Bridge from San Francisco. I've been assigned a cozy little room overlooking a birch grove. My roommate is a gentle soul who is frequently gone—he has a strong yen for sight-seeing. I'm not accustomed to being alone so much. I have only myself to get ready, one skinny single bed to make, one person's clothes to wash. I cannot physically pinpoint the feeling of loneliness; I ache all over.

I think it's time to *do* something rather than introspect: read, write, walk, talk, listen, discuss. I'll put away the mirrors which simply reflect and search for windows which open and reveal. Our enforced separation is giving me a chance to appreciate the people who love me.

I've been at San Francisco Theological Seminary two weeks now, and I'm faring better each new day. I actually whistled again, a sure sign of joy returning. When I picked up my mail, tucked in with Ellen's newsy note were greetings from the children, complete with artistic touches. David's creation almost did me in. In black crayon his message read, "Dear Dad, I miss you so much I cry in the night." I made a hasty exit from the mail room lest someone see my moistening eyes.

I get lonely quivers when I enter my bare room. There are no noisy greetings, no dogs jumping up and down, no pungent cooking smells to make my nose twitch, and no blaring television. Upon my return home, I hope I can remember its turmoil represents a vitality far more agreeable than the quiet emptiness I feel now.

I think I can. I think I can. I think I can—survive. The distance between us seems so great. And the pain of being left out of family events is acute. But it's the end of August; my time of return draws nigh.

I knew we could. I knew we could. I knew we could. Our reunion was sweet. I got showered with homemade confetti—high honor. I achieved reentry with limited gracefulness. Everyone's talking at once and trying to get a hug at the same time produced some friction. So be it. We made a safe and happy landing. It helped that I bore gifts from Chinatown and other exotic places.

In our highly mobile society, times of separation from loved ones are not uncommon. Knowing others experience the same pangs of loneliness may help, but the pain is still very real.

Making the effort to reach across the distance is important. I keep a journal to jot down significant events and experiences. When memory fades, I have a written record to assist my recollecting with loved ones and friends. And it's fun to review my notes and relive the experiences.

During my time of homesickness, I gained strength by meditating on Romans 8:38, 39:

> For I am persuaded, that neither death, nor life, nor angels, nor principalities, nor powers, nor things present, nor things to come, nor height, nor depth, nor any other creature, shall be able to separate us from the love of God, which is in Christ Jesus our Lord.

Yes, dads get lonely, too. We need the hugs and squeezes, and even the noise. But most of all, we need the love of God which is with us always and everywhere.

"Now our Lord Jesus Christ himself, and God, even our Father, which hath loved us, and hath given us everlasting consolation and good hope through grace, comfort your hearts, and stablish you in every good word and work" (2 Thess. 2:16, 17).

Sixteen

CUTE WINS EVERY TIME

How well I recall my mother's brave stand when I got my first dog. "No animal will *ever* set foot inside this house. And that's final!"

About a week later she pronounced, "Your dog can be in the kitchen, but I will not allow it on the living room rug. So don't ask."

After a month had passed, she drew her new line: "You keep that critter off the furniture, you hear?"

Her final utterance was, "I absolutely forbid that dirty mutt to sleep with you in bed."

Soon after, on my arrival home from school, whom do you suppose I found seated in her favorite chair with my soft, black puppy curled in her lap? I learned an important lesson: Intelligence is wonderful; strength is a plus; beauty is nice; but cute wins every time.

Cute is still a winner, particularly when it's spontaneous and not calculated. It possesses an irresistible attraction. A kitten draws people around who want to hold and pet it. They murmur, "Oh-h-h, isn't she cute?" This is exactly why we have two dogs. Steve brought home a stray after football practice. With her big brown eyes and all-over wiggle, how could we send her back into the cold, cruel world?

That's also why we're easy marks for donations to all kinds of youth activities. It's difficult, if not impossible, to tell an eager child, "No, I won't buy a ticket to your program." Even if we can't attend the function, it's an investment in the leadership of tomorrow. Also, fair is fair. We turn our children loose in the neighborhood to sell to folks such worthy commodities as Girl Scout cookies, soccer stickers, magazine subscriptions for school, and Little League candy bars.

I can send an encyclopedia salesman fleeing with a firm, "Not interested," but a small child standing on the step with a hopeful look melts me. Cute is hard to say no to. Can there be any other explanation of parents' willingness to change a baby's diapers or to wash a teenager's dirty socks?

This is apparently why God endowed human and animal infants with such appeal. At Lake Chelan for a short vacation, we observed a number of ducklings bobbing dutifully behind their respective mothers. There was one notable exception: a tiny puff of golden down which was either orphaned or lost. Duck mamas do not accept any babies except their own. This little fellow was in immediate danger of dying. We managed to corral it, bring it home, and build a duck house from a cardboard box. "Quacker" awoke us at 5:00 a.m. with its insistent cheep-cheeping. You'd better be cute if you rouse me at that hour of the day.

Quacker is now in his or her (we still haven't determined which denomination) third house. The latest design, a Kenmore washing machine box, rests on its side with chicken wire stretched across the opening. Several times each day, we take the duck out for a stroll, for swimming lessons, and for a feast of dandelion greens which annually prosper in our lawn. Nearly full grown, it quacks loudly and creates a disaster in the box, both to look at and to smell. If the creature weren't so cute, I'd buy a package of stuffing mix to go with the feast.

Ellen and I were running a bit late (as usual) on a spring afternoon that warmed us all the way to our bone marrow. On the corner of Washington and Emerson, a five-year-old girl was manning a Kool-Aid stand. An old end table served as the counter, and she sat on a wobbly apple box. A hand-painted sign advertised her product at five cents a glass. We drove by, glancing back all the while. "Oh, why not?" we said at the same time. "We're already late. What's another few minutes?"

At first nothing poured from her pitcher. Then adjusting the lid, half the contents splashed over the table and into her lap. We agreed to guard her business earnings, one lonely nickel, while she ran home to dry off. We felt a fifty-cent tip was in order. We're obviously suckers for children selling drinks by the roadside. How's a young person to learn the joys of free enterprise if no one will invest five cents?

Cute does win every time. I hope as we grow older, and perhaps wiser, we can retain some of our cuteness. I don't mean I want to act childishly. I refer to a capacity to believe in others, to expect good things to happen, and to live with zest. Some of the cutest folks I know have been that way over 65 years.

"Whatsoever things are lovely, whatsoever things are of good report; if there be any virtue, and if there be any praise, think on these things" (Phil. 4:8).

Seventeen

YOU'RE LUCKY, YOUR DAD'S A PREACHER

A school chum of Sara said to her, "Boy, you're lucky."
"Why do you think so?" Sara responded.
" 'Cause your dad's a preacher." Her friend assumed we preachers are perfect, never mad, upset or depressed. Perhaps she thinks Sara gets to do whatever Sara wants.

I hate to disillusion her, but we preachers are human just like everyone else, if not more so. Like all other fathers in the history of this planet, I must deal with the whole gamut of emotions and pressures. I've developed a system for coping which I call "A Cranky Dad's Lessons in Uncranking." It may not be perfect, but it works for me.

First, I've created my own little sanctuary in the corner of our bedroom. Sitting at my oak desk, I look out the window at the majestic hills. They're treeless but beautiful, changing color with the passing seasons. On one wall hangs a picture of a pixie-like man with red hair and a red beard, cradling a cute child in the crook of his arm. They're lying amid tall grass and wild flowers, pointing to puffy white clouds drifting overhead. These two dreamers are at peace. I'm helped by just glancing in their direction.

On my other side stands the speaker of our old stereo. I refer to it in the singular because only one speaker remains. The other one apparently was blown out from full-volume music played by an overly enthusiastic son or daughter. It works quite nicely for the volume I like, blocking out most competing noises.

As I sit there I can feel myself begin to relax. Soon the creative impulses are surging through my body (that may be a trifle overstated). Anyway, it's my very own spot where I can think my very own thoughts.

For therapy at a different pace, I don my grubby clothes and head for the garden or yard. Digging in the rich, brown earth is so basic that it calms my soul. It calls to the timeless rhythm of life, and helps me attune myself to all of creation. Better to do battle with aphids and to argue with morning glories than to fight with my family. I come back inside too dirty and tired to defend my selfish concerns. Very healthy, wouldn't you say?

Sometimes, I don't feel like doing work in any shape or form. Then I hunt down the basketball in its latest hiding place. I'm no Dr. J., but I can make it "around the world" and sink seven out of ten free throws. I dream of soaring through the air, weightless, to slam-dunk the ball. Since the spring in my legs was sprung long ago and my hands are too small to palm the ball, plus a multitude of other reasons, slam-dunking shall forever remain wishful thinking. Nevertheless, it's fun to pretend there are three seconds left in the championship game, I steal the ball, hurl a shot from half court, and . . .

Another beneficial habit for me is that of repeating calming thoughts, especially Scripture. "I can do all things through Christ which strengtheneth me" (Phil. 4:13). I usually do not quote it directly or accurately from the King James. That's incidental. The blessing comes when the message penetrates my head and heart. With Christ's strength I can get my work done before I go to bed, or survive Amy's slumber party, or make it through the myriad of problems confronting me. Paul doesn't write that I can do all things at once. It's enough to know that I'm not alone, that I have One who stands beside me always.

I'm a PK (preacher's kid). It was a mixture of blessing and bane, but the positive dimensions were far greater and more frequent. So many well-meaning people patted me on the head and asked if I were going to be a preacher, "just like your daddy," that

I rebelled. The more they inquired, the more I decided I wouldn't, not then, not ever. I changed.

Our six PK's are in the same stew. They're often in the public eye, partly because their dad uses them for sermon illustrations and writes books about them. They've handled the pressure with remarkable grace.

Life can be very lonely on a pedestal or in an ivory tower. I'd like people to know that I'm a people, too. I'm able to understand their joys and feel their sorrows. I hope they'll do the same for me and mine.

So, young friend of Sara, Sara is lucky. Her dad's got a job and it's one that lets him help a lot people. She's fortunate to have a secure home and to know she's loved very much. But even though Sara's dad may be a preacher, he's "real people."

"For if a man know not how to rule his own house, how shall he take care of the church of God?" (1 Tim. 3:5).

Eighteen

THEY ALSO SERVE WHO SIT ON THE BENCH

Our son Stephen is one of the best bench warmers I've ever witnessed. I mean that as a high compliment. He keeps interested and alert; his head and heart are in the game to the end. Other second-string players wander to the drinking fountain, watch clouds float by, or wave to friends in the stands. But Steve leads the cheers and walks in front of the coach frequently, ever hopeful. He doesn't do much warming in football, but in baseball he spends time on the sidelines. He knows not everyone can play all the time. Yet it's disappointing to be a spectator when his heart is set on being an active participant.

Nonetheless, Stephen was selected as a Babe Ruth League all-star. It was exciting stuff, complete with a colorful uniform and a classy new hat. There were also long practice sessions, causing sacrifices for him and us. He missed at least $200 in earnings from his summer job.

Mom and Dad journeyed to Moses Lake, seventy miles east, for the regional tournament. We figured he might not be a starter, but we hoped he'd enter in the later innings because of his excellent defensive skills. Such was not the case. His big moment was donning the catcher's mask to warm up the pitcher between innings three and four. Whoopee! Wenatchee (that's us) won the game, which brought a measure of comfort to us. Next day, we again were sitting on the hard, metal seats. Once again, our son sat on the bench. We're realists; we know he'll probably never play major-league ball. Still, every player chosen as an all-star deserves a chance to shine, if only for a few moments.

It was difficult to quietly watch him be overlooked, particularly when he was the only one of the roster with no game time. We were secretly happy his team lost their second game. Shame on us. But disappointment is not easy to handle gracefully. It just plain hurts, usually worse when it happens to a loved one instead of yourself.

We tried to bolster Steve's sagging ego. However, his drooping shoulders indicated his *inner* feelings. He played in the final two games, performing admirably (from a father's viewpoint).

Family life offers many joys, successes and happy experiences. It also inevitably brings disappointments. Our children will not always succeed. David had a tough time playing soccer. As the youngest team member, he felt like the scapegoat whenever something went wrong. But he stuck at it. He survived, though he shed a few tears.

Sara had labored all summer to save the twenty-seven dollars crammed inside her little brown purse. She cared for a neighbor's dog, faithfully brought in the mail and newspapers for a family on vacation, and rode her bicycle to feed her teacher's cat. She earned every penny. It was quite likely the most money she had ever accumulated. And was she proud! It was her very own, the product of hard work and perspiration. She felt so good being "rich" that she took her money to the mall. She had no intention of spending any. She just liked the feel of a purse stuffed with two tens, a five and her special two-dollar bill.

You may have guessed the outcome of this story: She lost her purse. We searched everywhere—in the car, around the yard, in her room. We turned the house upside down and inside out. No brown purse. No twenty-seven dollars. Sara cried for two hours. Ellen and I considered staging a fake recovery, but we couldn't do it. There was only one purse like hers in the entire world. Brother Steve generously volunteered to replace her loss with hard-earned money of his own. Ellen and I gave her the money and attempted to assuage her sorrow. I wished I had been the one who'd lost it.

Perhaps the hardest thing to deal with is a family member letting another down. Dad fails to make good on a promise; a child defies a rule or value we've tried hard to establish; one of us fails to do his best. It hurts.

What's to be done? Keep going; keep plugging; keep believing in each other. Though my children disappoint me a thousand times, I shall continue rooting for them, no matter how many games they sit on the bench, no matter how many mistakes they make, no matter how many purses they lose. Steadfastness is a key to being a successful family.

I want them to know the future is wide open. There will be other games, new opportunities, fresh chances. But I still think Steve should have played more, even if they'd only stuck him in right field.

"Bless them which persecute you: bless, and curse not. Rejoice with them that do rejoice, and weep with them that weep" (Rom. 12:14, 15).

Nineteen

THE ENDS WILL NEVER MEET

As most families, we struggle to make ends meet. At certain times of the year the effort assumes epic dimensions. Stephen and Amy have birthdays at the end of August and school begins soon thereafter. Do you know how much six pairs of shoes cost? Plus school supplies: pens, pencils, erasers, notebooks? Plus shirts, blouses, sweaters, socks, and jeans? Plus winter coats (stores have sales during August)? Plus student activity cards, school pictures, insurance, and high-school yearbook fees? Plus milk money, lunch sacks, barbecue chips and Twinkies? By the end of September our family's financial ends are so far apart they may never get back together. If they should ever come within shouting distance, we'd have to reintroduce them.

It's an anxiety producing dilemma, no doubt common to 99% of humanity, but still scary. Somehow we make it through the end of each month to greet the advent of the next. But there's hardly time to catch our breaths before the ends start pulling apart again. As a result, I'm not certain if our younger children know what a fancy steak is. And they are realizing there is a limited number of creative ways to fix hot dogs. We're waiting for some clever person to publish a cookbook on 101 wiener recipes. But eating meat at our place may end entirely if we don't do a better job of making ends meet.

On the other hand, so what if there aren't enough funds to go around? What else is new? Families in caves, teepees, and log cabins probably experienced the same thing. Why should it be any different for us today? As responsible persons, we can scale down our expectations, concentrate our spending on keeping the kids healthy and well-nourished, and just enjoy life in between those pesky ends.

Okay, I admit it. We splurge once in a while. We go to lunch someplace ritzier than we should, buy an article of clothing we don't absolutely need, see a movie everybody's talking about, or do something really daring like purchase a rich chocolate bar while waiting in line at the grocery store checkout stand. Grocery store managers are going to be judged for displaying gum, candy, trashy newspapers, and other nonessentials by the cash registers. They prey on the weaknesses of good folk like me. The other evening I came home with bread, paper towels, cheese, beef noodle soup, a gallon of milk, and *two* Swiss Chocolate Almond bars. After all, I had to stand there staring at the piles of junk food. I couldn't help it. I yielded. I started out with strength, but have you ever had to inhale the smell of chocolate for ten minutes?

We are not going to panic. But we are teetering on the brink. If it were only the financial ends that resisted meeting, it wouldn't be quite so traumatic. It's all those other ends as well: the amount of available time and the number of jobs demanding attention, the work piled on my desk and my level of energy, what I'm suppose to remember and what my memory bank is capable of retaining.

I *must* not yield to panic. True, I'll never catch up, let alone get ahead—not on my work schedule, sleep, finances, or anything else. But maybe that's a good sign. Could it mean I'm needed and important, that I'm not on a shelf gathering dust and cobwebs? Am I like Sisyphus in Greek mythology, who could never push his rock to the top. Am I forever trying to hook ends together that shall never quite connect?

So much for philosophizing. There isn't time to sit and reflect right now. I must walk home tonight, and if I don't get started, I'll miss dinner. You see, we're a one-car family—temporarily, I hope.

The little Fiat sputtered, gasped and died—in the middle of a busy street, of course. The electric fuel pump had decided to quit doing its appointed task. And since the shop doesn't have the correct replacement part and must order one from goodness-knows-where, I'm walking. It might be a well-camouflaged blessing. When I walk, I feel better from the exercise, and I observe things I would never see if I were speeding by in the car. I notice butterflies and rosebuds. I see blades of grass bravely poking through sidewalk cracks. I smell fresh air, a newly-mown lawn, the nearby bakery, and the sagebrush which is so pungent after a rainstorm in the surrounding hills. I see people, not just windshields and bumpers. I see faces and bodies, smiles and frowns. Perhaps I've been moving too rapidly trying frantically to bring together all the loose ends. I have missed many of the joys and pleasures all around me.

The more money we have, the more bills there are. The more time I have at my disposal, the greater the demands upon it. I'm attempting to accept the fact that the ends will never meet. But God promises us the strength to carry on, to keep reaching out, and to continue growing as we tackle the challenges.

My life as a person and a parent bears no certificate, Satisfaction Guaranteed. I won't get any money back; what I've spent is gone, I hope wisely invested. There is no promise of trouble-free usage; I shall have to fix things and repair relationships as needed. There is no assurance of success, just ample opportunities to learn from mistakes.

Who cares if the ends never meet? That's their problem, not mine. My life has been linked to that of the Master. I'm part of His beautiful family. What more could a person ask?

"Therefore take no thought, saying, What shall we eat? or, What shall we drink? or, Wherewithal shall we be clothed? . . . for your heavenly Father knoweth that ye have need of all these things. But seek ye first the kingdom of God, and his righteousness; and all these things shall be added unto you" (Matt. 6:31–33).

Twenty

THE ART OF WAITING

I'm doing it again—waiting. I think I've spent half this week waiting. I've waited at the dentist's office; at the drive-through bank (as usual, I chose the wrong line behind two customers with complicated transactions); at the church—for parents to pick up their youngsters following a youth gathering. I've waited for a couple to arrive at a marriage counseling session, for the same couple at their wedding rehearsal, and for the best man on the wedding day. As a matter of fact, I'm writing this chapter while waiting at the bus depot for the next Greyhound to Seattle.

I wouldn't dare list all the times, places and occasions I've waited for our children. But allow me to share a representative sampling:

- Cooled my heels eleven minutes at the junior high school while Amy finished drill team practice.
- Sat on hard, splintery bleachers for an hour for one Babe Ruth baseball game to end so our son's team could take the field.
- Slouched in the car (with the engine running) while two daughters said good-bye after spending the night with cousins Angie and Jill.
- Twiddled my thumbs twelve minutes while Steve finished a weight-lifting routine at high school.
- Fidgeted for over two hours at a track meet before our daughter's scheduled events: the 100-meter dash and the 400-meter relay.

- Sat at the dinner table with the food growing cold and stomach growling, waiting for everybody to hush so we could offer thanks.

To make things worse, for half the phone calls I've made this week, I've been put on hold (the interminable type where they punch the button and go for coffee).

Children have a special sixth sense enabling them to know precisely when it's most inconvenient for parents to wait. They're seldom late when we have time to spare. But let us be in a rush, and sure enough, they're long overdue. For example, at the agreed upon time, I arrived at the school to pick up John. With two evening meetings yet to attend, plus a home visit to make, I was in a hurry. Five minutes elasped—no John on the horizon. Ten minutes—I was barely resisting the urge to honk the horn in staccato rhythm. Other students had long since left and gone home. Finally, I caught his familiar amble in the rearview mirror. He climbed in and plopped his books on the seat. "Come on, Dad, get going! I'm starved." I gave him a squinty-eyed glance as I pulled out of the parking lot.

Waiting *with* children can be even more exciting. While Mom tries things on in the fitting room of a clothing store, Dad gets the honor of watching the troops. First, one escapes and crawls under the nearest clothes rack. I can tell where he or she is hiding by watching garments fall from their hangers. Another child is breathing heavily on a full-length mirror and writing his name in the mist. The store's automatic door opener is being field-tested by a third little person. "How long does it take," I murmur, "to find out if a dress fits?"

Wouldn't it be grand if it were possible to stockpile or invest the time spent waiting? Then, in a situation when time runs short and panic lurks close by, I could withdraw fifteen minutes from my account. Nevertheless, I'd probably procrastinate and still be in a dither the final few minutes.

I've conducted an informal survey of the ways people deal with waiting. Folks jingle their keyrings, chew their fingernails, twiddle thumbs, pace back and forth, or sit and fidget. It's a wonderful opportunity to perfect their nervous twitches. Others simply collapse with sighs or take naps. Young couples often snuggle. Children explore (if given freedom) or squirm (if they're not). Many converse if they are fortunate enough to be with friends. Some people fill the space by reading. In spite of all the methods of dealing with waiting, irritation and anger often poke up their ugly heads. "It is good that a man should both hope and quietly wait for the salvation of the Lord" (Lam. 3:26). The text should include an asterisk exempting parents who are waiting for a loitering child.

"Who does he think he is, making me wait like this? I'm busy!"

"I don't have time for this nonsense. She'd better get a move on, or else." I can never figure out what the "or else" might be. It just sounds good to attach that phrase to the end of a parental threat.

"Why is it always *me* who has to wait?" The answer to this question is clear. Anyone who serves (including a parent) not only waits *on* others but also *for* them.

Waiting is a difficult art to master. It's work which demands emotional energy and creativity. The minutes creep by while I wait. The longest hour I ever endured was in a hospital lobby when Ellen was birthing homegrown child number one. I went with her into the delivery room on the next two occasions, not only to be part of the process, but because I couldn't stand the suspense.

Perhaps it's a matter of justice. Over the years, I've made my share of people wait. As a child and youth, I took it for granted that my parents would wait for me, no matter what. Well, I'm now receiving my just reward.

I have a long way to go before I perfect the art of waiting. But if I have many more weeks like this one, I'll soon be ready to do a masterpiece.

"The patient in spirit is better than the proud in spirit" (Eccles. 7:8).

Twenty-one

THE HANDY DAD CAN

I battled with pipe wrenches today. I eventually won, but what a fight! Grandpa and Grandma were being thoughtful when they gave us a new faucet for the kitchen sink as a Christmas present. How were they to envision the mortal struggle which would ensue? I plumb about once every two years, and consequently forget everything I have previously learned, which isn't much.

I assembled the necessary tools: pliers, Phillips screwdriver, pipe wrenches, and a hammer. A hammer is a very useful plumbing tool: pounding on something relieves tension. I actually read the instructions before beginning. Then I tackled removing the old faucet and spray hose. Parts of it were stuck so tightly they required a lot of muscle power. And the hammer.

I was lying on my back under the sink, in a puddle of water (naturally), looking up and getting specks of rust in my eyes. I heard the sound of running water, close by. "Oh-oh," I muttered, as my back became sopping wet. The trap on the drain had collapsed. Over the years, the bottom section of the J-shaped pipe had corroded until only the metallic silver coating was left.

I cleaned up the mess and myself, then hurried to the hardware store. I took the old trap along to be certain I chose the correct size. It went smoothly. I felt smug about being so clever and handy. If "a haughty spirit goeth before a fall," then smug goeth before a catastrophe. I put the new trap in place, but it wouldn't quite fit until I had disconnected another piece of pipe, then another. When it was neatly reassembled, I turned on the water to check for leaks; sure enough, I found several. I believe that water leaks for the pure joy of it. Groseclose's Law of Plumbing is: "When I plumb, water finds somewhere to leak; when I fix that leak, it finds two other spots; then there are four drips, and so forth, *ad infinitum.*"

Back to the faucet. The new one had shorter copper tubing than the old one, so down to my friendly hardware store again for two lengths of flexible tubing. I forgot to take along the fitting. Though I had carefully measured the length, I neglected to check the diameter. I decided to live dangerously and buy half-inch. It was the last correct thing I would do for some time.

As an aside to this whole fiasco, I should tell you that I had not yet shaved, and my hair was matted and my hands smudged. On both visits to town, I encountered a multitude of parishioners. It never fails. If I go shopping dressed to the hilt, nobody sees me. But let me go out looking my worst, and half the congregation is there.

I returned home, hooked the pipes together, tightened every connection, and turned on the water. Beautiful. Then I tried to turn the faucet off. Cold water kept pouring out full speed. I tried everything (except the hammer). At that moment, the drain pipe decided to spring a new leak. I fixed the drain, removed the new faucet, mopped the floor, and drove across town to the store where Grandpa and Grandma had bought the faucet. The salesman was kind and, more importantly, knowledgeable. He immediately knew the source of the problem. He made a minor adjustment and said, "There, it'll work perfectly—no problem."

No problem! I thought. No problem! What does he know? For five hours I've been struggling and arguing. I've missed lunch, my back is sore, I've broken a fingernail, and he has the gall to say, "No problem." It was probably fortunate for both of us I didn't have the hammer in my hand.

I am now upstairs writing this sad tale. I'm not making much progress because I must stop typing every few moments to listen for the sound of dripping water. The kids haven't come up to the bathtub to get boats and rubber ducks, so there must not be a flood.

We parents have a constant parade of broken things needing repair. The following is a partial list of my recent repair jobs. It is not intended to impress, but to inspire.

- Resoldered Amy's antenna on her radio.
- Tied the clothes hamper frame together after the weight of dirty clothes bent it in two.
- Replaced the plug on Steve's blow dryer. It had been pulled out by the roots once too often. One of the prongs was stuck in the outlet, so I had to turn off the power to pull it out. Therefore the digital clocks reverted to 12:00 and had to be reset.
- A hose on the swimming pool sprang a leak. It was tricky trying to change hoses without draining the pool; Ellen's quick hands helped.
- Replaced a pane of glass in the door because the old one broke when the door was slammed. The door was slammed because the knob was jammed. The knob was jammed because it had been turned a thousand times per day (minimum).

My present work list includes reinstalling a towel bar on the wall and repairing the shower stall where John slipped. He bent over to wash his feet, stepped on a bar of soap, and fell through the side of the stall. The hole is covered with contact paper while I gather my courage to refit tile.

I'm not likely to make it into the Handyman's Hall of Fame. My problem isn't a lack of skill. I just don't have the right tools. Every craftsperson knows he needs the right tools for the job. It requires more than a hammer.

"He [Christ] is before all things, and in him all things hold together" (Col. 1:17, RSV).

Twenty-two

NOW THAT I HAVE YOUR ATTENTION

Our church has an 8:00 a.m. outdoor service during the summer months. We use a small, flatbed trailer holding the electric piano, the sound system, the pulpit and me. One rainy Sunday morning we rigged a plastic canopy to shelter the crew on the trailer. I was earnestly praying, when the weight of the water on the canopy above me caused a two-by-four to fall. The board struck me alongside the head, "Thunk!"

I continued my prayer. "Lord, now that you have my attention, what is it you want to tell me?"

I know how God must feel at times. Until I gain a person's attention, I might as well talk to the wall. I simply will not get a response.

Years ago, Ellen and I were afraid our second son had impaired hearing. We tried talking loudly when issuing commands, but with no results. We enunciated very clearly when asking him questions. We received blank looks. One day, when his back was turned and he was across the room, I whispered, "Do you want a cookie?" He wheeled around immediately.

"You bet! What kind? How many may I have?" He had betrayed a classic case of selective listening, of hearing only what he wanted, and nothing more.

We parents have different methods of combatting this practice. I spread my body in front of the television screen to gain their undivided attention. They crane their necks this way and that, trying to see their favorite show.

"Hey, guys, did it occur to you that I might be blocking your view because I want to talk with you?"

"Sure, Dad, but could you move for a minute? The best part is on right now. We'll talk during the next commercial."

That's when I reach back, push the "off" button, and reply, "Sorry, I'm going to talk now." If you ever wish to observe the symptoms of impatience, this is the moment to take good notes. The kids squirm and fidget; I believe the contemporary phrase is, "They get antsy." I've barely finished my speech before the show is back on and their eyes are riveted to the TV again. Did they really hear? Or were they only pretending so I'd hurry and quit talking?

Another of my attention-getting tricks is the use of empty threats. "If you don't listen to what I've got to say, you'll be in big trouble." I find it a challenge to create new, more effective threats. Familiarity breeds indifference, so we parents are duty bound to create new warnings. "You can't go anywhere, and I mean *anywhere*, until you clean that disaster area you call a room."

"Oh, good, no more school for me."

"No, no, I mean out to play, or to shop or to see a movie— the fun things you do."

"You admit it, then. School isn't any fun?"

"I didn't say that. You're putting words in my mouth. There are some enjoyable activities at school."

"Name one, besides lunch and recess."

They're so clever with words, I wonder why more young people don't grow up to become lawyers. John, 17, is our best example.

One day I said, "John, I thought we told you to finish your homework before you went to the bowling alley."

"Oh, were you talking to me?"

"You were the only one who wanted to go bowling. So why are your books still on the floor where you threw them?"

"They aren't."

"It sure looks like it to me."

"No, Dad, I kicked them with my foot on the way out the door, so they aren't quite in the same place."

"Stop mincing words and give me straight answers. You were supposed to do that homework."

"Sorry, Dad, my mistake. I guess I misunderstood. I call it schoolwork. I thought you meant something around the house, and I'd already done all of that."

"You knew good and well what I meant. Don't give me any more excuses."

"They aren't excuses."

"Call them whatever you want, son: legitimate reasons, extenuating circumstances, temporary incompetence. As far as I'm concerned, they're excuses. You messed up, and that's that. I won't stand for this anymore." If I'd had a white flag, I'd have waved it vigorously at this point.

When all else has failed (please note: I did not say "if"), I talk a bit more loudly. Actually, I yell. I try very hard not to raise my voice. I really do. It's just that after being ignored and/or grossly misinterpreted, I become upset. Out comes my preacher voice reverberating through the house.

I do get perturbed at myself when I yield to the urge to yell. And I frequently direct a brief pep talk to my own soul: "You are the adult person, remember? And they are the children. You should act more rationally and calmly. Take it easy, relax, breathe deeply, and talk quietly." It works for all of a minute.

I might do well to borrow a line by the late John Wayne. While standing tall, he firmly declared, "Listen, pilgrim, and listen tight." Folks perked up their ears when he spoke. Of course, those six shooters strapped on his hips and that star pinned to his massive chest probably helped.

Actually, I have a wonderful model close at hand, my own father. When he quit smiling, I knew it was time to "listen tight," to fly right. There were no empty threats, no word games, no yelling. Maybe I'd better do some more homework in the field of parenting.

One additional thing I've noticed. It helps immensely if once I get their attention, I have something worthwhile to say. I'd appreciate it if you'd keep me in your prayers.

"Wherefore, my beloved brethren, let every man be swift to hear, slow to speak, slow to wrath" (James 1:19).

Twenty-three

"PICK A LITTLE, TALK A LITTLE, CHEEP, CHEEP, CHEEP"

In Rodger's and Hammerstein's *The Music Man*, a group of ladies gathers regularly to knit and quilt, or whatever women of that era did. But the real reason they got together was to gossip about the goings on in River City. They sang a clever song, "Pick a Little, Talk a Little, Cheep, Cheep, Cheep." Replace those Iowa ladies with our family members and the lyrics remain basically the same. We pick a little, talk a little, cheep, cheep, blah, blah, yakkity-yak.

Frequently, we don't just pick a little, we pick a lot.

"Stop slouching and stand up straight."

"You're not wearing those holey-kneed pants to school."

"Stop chewing your fingernails."

"Eat your string beans, drink your milk, use your napkin." Pick, pick, pick. Cheep, cheep, cheep.

The messy state of their rooms is a source of major discussion. "Dad, it's my room! If I don't care what it looks like, why should you?"

"Because it's our home, and there are minimum standards which we all must meet. So get busy and clean that disaster area before you watch any more television."

Sometimes my nagging must sound like a broken record to them.

Get it done faster.
Be neater and more polite.
Don't talk and chew at the same time.
Where are you going?
Where have you been?
Put gas in the tank yourself.
Turn the radio down.
Get off the telephone.

Do I seem like a drill sergeant who barks nonstop orders? Do my children feel as though they can never quite measure up? It's a delicate balance. I want them to understand our love is not based on performance. We will accept them whether they receive an "A" or an "F." We won't be pleased about the latter grade because they are capable of better. We are called to encourage them, not to pick, nag, and go cheep, cheep, cheep.

I admit I'm a virtuoso whiner. When I blast forth fatherly commands, and my troops fail to come to attention and salute, I often start whining. I'm not loud about it. My voice just acquires an impatient edge. It is not a productive habit. I'm afraid all it teaches them is how to whine right back.

It's not hard to borrow trouble. There's always someone who'll lend you as much as you want and at whatever terms you wish. When I whine at them I'm usually not so much upset with them as with myself. When I'm at peace in my soul, I do far more praising than picking.

Why I behave as I do is something of a mystery to me. We may have ten wonderful family experiences in a row. Then up crops a conflict. We pick and cheep at each other, and that one unpleasant event dominates my thinking. I let it crowd out all the happy feelings. I ought to remind myself of the ratio. Ten-to-one odds are fabulous!

Another source of parental picking revolves around personal hygiene and outward appearances: too much dirt at age four; too much eye shadow or lipstick at fourteen. Even if you don't know their precise age, you can tell when they become teenagers. Until that time, you can't get them to take a shower. After they turn thirteen, you can't get them out of the shower. Thank goodness for fast-recovery water heaters. To estimate the number of teengers in a house, simply total the number of hair dryers, hot-air combs, curling irons, and complexion creams and divide by three. I've concluded that cleanliness has little to do with godliness and everything to do with having noticed the opposite sex.

I question the validity of using chronological age to measure a person's maturity. It would be more accurate to take the median level of behavior. On some days, a fifteen-year-old acts like a grown-up, yet the very next day like an immature nine-year-old. The only difference in calculating a middle-aged person's average behavior is the spread of the numbers. My maturity level is calculated by adding a childish six and a weary eighty and dividing by two.

This problem of picking could be helped greatly if an architectural genius would design a house that could be changed as the family grew older and larger. Small children require constant visual contact. Parents need to hear what they're up to and see what they're into. The little ones need reassurance that Mom or Dad is close by. Somewhere, somehow, this all changes. By the teen years, they don't want their moves monitored. The same goes double for the parents who would rather not listen to their teenagers' music, look in their rooms, or watch them preen before the mirror.

Open spaces needed for toddlers could have soundproof dividers added for teens. Doors that remained constantly open would receive locks to insure privacy. One telephone which was once adequate would be worn out if another wasn't purchased. A family room would undergo a metamorphosis from rocking horses and Fisher-Price toys to video games and pool tables.

Whatever the condition of their rooms, whether they take thirty-minute showers, thirty-second showers, or no showers at all, it's crucial we talk kindly often and pick as little as possible. I shall let the birds do the cheeping and leave the whining to our dogs when they ask to be let outside.

"Pleasant words are as a honeycomb, sweet to the soul, and health to the bones" (Prov. 16:24).

Twenty-four

I'VE DONE MY SHARE

I usually sputter and fuss as I pick up the mess in the front yard. Clutter in the backyard doesn't bother me much, but when it's right there for the whole neighborhood to see, I get uptight. My problem has grown since the folks next door retired. They now have time to keep their place immaculately groomed. They walk around looking for things to do. I try *not* to see all the work that needs to be done in my yard.

Back to my tidying up. I dump the baseball gloves and bats in the apple box we use for sports equipment. I flip the Frisbee on the porch on my second try—my first throw landed in the bushes. Loaded with all the stuff the kids dumped out of the tree house, I struggle up the ladder and stash it again. I roll four bicycles into the garage, and move a pair of roller skates before closing the door. I rescue the basketball from the pumpkin vine where it has somehow strayed.

Do Ellen and I have to put everything away around this house? Can't anybody else remember to do his part? If creation is to remain orderly, it all depends on us parents. I feel as though we're the designated picker-uppers of the universe. I suppose I could leave things right where they fall. But I couldn't stand it. I was brought up to believe that everything has a place, and there's a place for everything. I also worry, justifiably so, that toys and equipment may be stolen.

A frequently heard conversation between Ellen or me and the kids goes like this: "Hey, after you're done playing, don't forget to pick up."

"Oh, sure, Dad. We'll do it. You can relax to the max."

Several hours elapse, and I notice (surprise! surprise!) that nothing has been tidied.

"Didn't I tell you to clean the place before you watched televison?"

"Yeah, but we're tired. We'll do it later." Funny thing—I've seldom seen "later" arrive at our house.

After a long day of working at the office, transporting children hither and yon, straightening the yard, washing and folding clothes and fixing dinner, Ellen and I feel like answering the next request, "Sorry, we're off duty. We've done our share today and we're going to relax (or maybe totally collapse)."

"But it won't take a minute," they would solemnly assure us.

Ha! We've heard that line too many times to be suckered.

Often when we're working around the house, one of our children will say, "I already vacuumed the family room. I've done my share. Make John dust the shelves. He hasn't worked as hard as I have." Sigh. She's probably right. John didn't do as much. I had seen him sneak into his room to finish reading a Western he hadn't wanted to put down.

I may have done my share and met my obligations. But is that all the Lord desires of me as a spouse, parent, or employer/employee? When I say, "I've done my share," am I limiting my usefulness to God? Am I staring at the minimum when I ought to be stretching to do the maximum?

It's not particularly helpful for me to keep track of all the tasks I've done around the house—"This is the third time in two days I've had to mop the kitchen floor. Somebody keeps spilling juice. Now hear this: use two hands on the pitcher."

"We can't," one of them replies. "We have to hold the glass with the other hand and keep the refrigerator door open with our elbow."

I advise, "You could shut the refrigerator door and pour your drink at he counter." Apparently, such a logical approach never occurs to them.

I recently had a discussion with the Lord about this situation. "Lord," I asked, "what are my duties as a father?"

"You know the requirements," He replied. "You are to provide food and shelter, clothing and transportation. See to it that they receive a good education, and train them in spiritual matters."

"These things have I faithfully done since our first child was born," I answered. "I've been doing my share all along."

"So you have. Yet, I don't think you know what 'my share' really means. Your share is neither a prescribed amount of work nor hours on the job. Your share is to do what you are capable of doing, to love and serve with the strength I give you. You would be a better parent, my son, and a happier person, too, if you'd quit keeping track of your share. Actually, I don't want you to do your share. I want you to give your whole self."

I added a meek "Amen."

How sweet it is when the family is working together and no one says (or even thinks) about who has worked harder, done more, or had a tougher job. It's wonderful when we all pitch in just for the joys of fellowship and accomplishment.

If I have the energy and can find time, then the task is part of my share. May I constantly remember, with thankfulness, that God kept on giving to me long after He'd done His share. He didn't stop at merely creating a useful world; He lavished this earth with beauty and majesty. He didn't simply bring me into existence as a physical being; He offered me an inner life of the spirit, of peace and love and joy.

God could have said, "I've done more than enough already, why should I send my Son? Let them figure a way out of their own predicament." But in His abounding grace, He gave us Jesus, the Word become flesh.

I shall try to fulfill my calling and pass on God's blessings. I have certainly received more than "my share."

"And if any man will sue thee at the law, and take away thy coat, let him have thy cloke also. And whosoever shall compel thee to go a mile, go with him twain" (Matt. 5:40, 41).

Twenty-five

IF I'M THE HEAD OF THE HOUSEHOLD, WHY AM I AT THE BACK OF THE PACK?

No less an authority than Holy Writ charges me to be the leader of my family (Eph. 5, 6). A profusion of books on marriage and family living emphasize the headship role of the father. Well, if I'm the head of this whole show, how come I'm usually at the end of the line, the last one to get into the bathroom, and the final person to get fed? The only person I ever beat is Ellen.

I prefer to think it's not the ravages of age slowing us down. The reason Ellen and I are at the back of the pack is simple: somebody needs to herd stragglers and to pick up stray sneakers, dirty clothes, hair curlers, wet towels, and candy bar wrappers. I doubt our children wander farther or drop more than the national average. Yet it seems to require our constant vigilance to maintain a semi-tidy and relatively orderly household.

A case in point is our relationship with the secretarial staff at the junior high. During the past few years, they have been privileged to make and remake our acquaintance. We have trudged to the office several times each week bearing left-behind lunches, forgotten homework assignments, P.E. shorts, textbooks, and the like. We've now graduated to high shcool. When I approach the counter I don't say anything. The person on duty smiles knowingly (it borders on a smirk). "Is this for you-know-who?" they ask. I nod affirmatively, deposit the article, and head back to whatever prior task I'd been attempting to accomplish—if I can still remember what it was.

Somebody must tag along behind to pick up the pieces, sweep the crumbs, and remove what's strewn on the floor. While I'm on the subject, there seem to be contradictory definitions of the word "floor." I've always assumed floors were for standing on, for arranging furniture upon, and for providing passageways from one room to another. Young people apparently function under totally different assumptions. If there were a teen dictionary, the listing might be as follows:

> floor /flôr/ *n*. 1: a flat surface designed to catch whatever is dropped, thrown, or otherwise not placed where it belongs. 2: that area of the room purported to exist beneath piles of dirty clothes, papers, and other assorted clutter. 3: what parents think they've been knocked to when they glance inside their teen-age son's or daughter's room.

However, it is possible for us to lead from the back of the pack, and it's absolutely essential. Children progress rapidly from unsteady toddlers to flashy speedsters. There is no way this dad can hope to keep pace, let alone stay out front. When we go shopping, for example, I like to carefully examine the merchandise and the price tags. When we go for a walk, I enjoy a leisurely stroll. Not them; they ricochet along, bouncing from one fascinating distraction to another.

Perhaps it's due to a change in body chemistry. Following a meal, my adult body feels quite mellow. I hunt for a quiet, cozy corner where I can curl up. But a child seems to convert the same food into instant energy. He has a desperate need to burn it off immediately. This metabolic difference is a source of potential conflict.

Here's the plot. I had just gorged myself on ham and scalloped potatoes when a young voice yelled, "Dad, we need you to referee our wiffelball game. Steve's not being fair!" I rose from the couch in slow motion. Outside, the fresh air cleared my senses after a few deep gasps, and agitated voices awakened my ears.

"STRI-I-IKE!" I exclaimed.

"No way, Dad," complained the batter. "That was a mile outside,"

"BALL ONE," I hollered on the next pitch.

John glowered from his pitching spot. "What? You called that a ball? It was right down the middle. Uh-h-h, maybe Steve should umpire again."

"Yeah," added another child. "He calls 'em better than you do, Dad."

"Too bad, guys. I'm wide awake now. And for your information, the first pitch was over the corner of the plate and the second was low. PLAY BALL!"—"That's STRI-I-IKE TWO!" More moans and groans.

I'm thankful that being the head of the household doesn't mean I always have to be in front. Dad doesn't have to be first in line to command their attention and respect. I recall Jesus, our Lord and Master, who knelt humbly before each disciple to wash his feet; who came not to be served but to serve (Matt. 20:28); who derived His authority from above and not by being out front all the time. Because Jesus knew He'd soon be leaving His followers, He wanted to give them an illustration of godly leadership and thus equip them to take initiative.

I, too, know that my family will eventually be leaving the nest. I want them to be prepared. If they have learned my values, I don't have to be leading them visibly. The time comes quite early in their lives when Ellen and I cannot be physically present to make decisions for them. But if the heart-ties are there, and if they know what God's standards are, they'll be able to make wise choices.

Yes, they'll stray occasionally. Their bedroom floors won't miraculously be clean. Every so often, the shower curtain will end up outside the tub when the water's running. But I really don't mind trailing along behind to herd my little flock, to pick up after them, or to mop the bathroom. I'm secure in the knowledge that I'm the head of this household. Now, if the rest of the people around here could just get the message. . . .

"And, behold, there are last which shall be first, and there are first which shall be last" (Luke 13:30).

Twenty-six

THE BAFFLING CASE OF THE "WHAT IF'S"

Our family is off to northern Idaho for a mini-vacation, all
except John and Steve. We're leaving them home for the weekend. The two boys ought to be capable of surviving for three days.
John's seventeen and Steve is nearly sixteen. They know how to
cook their favorite foods: vegetable beef soup, TV dinners, frozen
pizza, and popcorn. They won't starve.

So why are we worrying? Why are we afflicted with a bad case
of the "what if's"? What if they forget to turn off the stove? What
if they let the dogs escape from the backyard? What if they leave
the television on all night? What it they don't shut the freezer door
or put the milk away? What if... We could make a list of "what
if's," but it would boggle their minds.

Instead, we tried the old method of "lecture and remind." They
became as weary of listening as we did of talking. Finally, we
hushed up and switched to silent prayer and quiet worry.

"Lord, we've got to trust them. They'll do just fine, won't they?
After all, they are growing up. But what if the hot water heater
springs a leak? What if the house burns down? What if the sky
should fall ?"

As a final gesture, we left little notes in strategic places: a
suggested menu on the kitchen cupboard, "Turn off the oven"
on the stove top, directions for feeding our various pets, phone

numbers in case of emergency, and so forth. The house was plastered with helpful hints and suggestions.

Lord knows, there are a multitude of concerns that cause parents to ask, "What if?" When our children were small, I wondered, what if he or she gets lost?

With John now driving a car, I have added some new "what if's" to my inventory. What if he gets a ticket? What if he runs out of gas? What if he has an accident?

When our children moved from grade school into junior high, I thought they were more likely to encounter the problems of the big world. What if classmates offer them drugs or invite them to parties where the alcohol flows and sexual promiscuity is the norm?

Then there's Steve, who though strong and agile, is still a bit light for high-school football. Is his neck strong enough? What if he gets hurt? I can see why parents try to tie their progeny to those proverbial apron strings.

The beat goes on. Last spring, when Amy tried out for the junior high drill team, I, in the worst way, wanted her to be chosen. She certainly had enough energy and was quite well-coordinated. But I was afraid she wouldn't make it. A lot of subjective criteria would enter the selection process. So I stewed—what if she doesn't make it? Will it damage her self-image? Will it strain her peer relationships?

She was chosen. Now I'm asking a different set of questions. What if we can't afford all the outfits she needs, the shoes, gloves, knee socks, and sweaters? We probably can't afford it, yet for her sake, we can't afford not to. And Amy has been terrific about using her babysitting money to help defray expenses.

Why are the majority of "what if" questions negative, pointing out unhappy possibilities? Perhaps it indicates a lack of trust in one another and in God. Let's hear it for "what if's" of a positive nature. For example, what if they make the honor roll or do their jobs around home without being nagged? What if they date a young person with high moral values? If parents' attitudes were more hopeful, anticipating good results, then children might strive harder to measure up to those expectations.

By the way, John and Steve did survive the weekend. Friday

evening's chili burned in the pan from being cooked on high heat so they substituted breakfast bars and cereal, and Steve spent Saturday morning scrubbing the black off the pan. John left the milk out overnight, but Steve drank it anyway. The house was still standing; the pets were healthy. Maybe next time we'll have more confidence in their abilities.

But what if they forget to lock the house at night? What if. . .?

"Don't worry about anything; instead, pray about every-thing; tell God your needs and don't forget to thank him for his answers. If you do this you will experience God's peace, which is far more wonderful than the human mind can understand" (Phil. 4:6, 7a, TLB).

Twenty-seven

TEMPERED, NOT TANTRUMMED

I would like to blame the bean-with-bacon soup. As is his custom, Steve filled his bowl to the brim. Amy, the meal's chef, informed him in no uncertain terms that he had taken more than his share. "Steve, leave enough for me and for Mom and Dad."

"I will, Amy!" he snapped. "Why don't you just bug off?"

"I don't have to. I'm the one who cooked the soup."

"Big deal! You aren't my mom."

"I never said I was. Besides, that'd be the worst job in the whole world." At this juncture the real mom arrived on the scene to restore order. During this relatively minor altercation, I had been working downstairs, safely removed from the fray. But when Steve's loud voice continued to filter down the stairwell, I decided it was time for Dad to take charge and solve the problem.

A heated, rather irrational argument ensued between two males with ruffled feathers. Ellen threw up her hands in despair; Amy plugged her ears. Finally, Steve left his full bowl and returned to watch television, muttering that he wasn't hungry anymore. I escaped back to my office to try to calm down.

After a suitable cooling-off period, Ellen called me up for soup and crackers. She informed me that Amy had cooked it especially for me. So I ate bean with bacon soup at 2:30 in the afternoon. The thick, reheated soup tasted great.

Thankfully, such outbursts don't happen often around our house. Tantrums are never helpful because they're so self-centered. It doesn't matter whether the culprit is a "terrible two" or a "flagrant forty." It's not enlightening at all.

I wonder, then, why don't I quit having my little tantrums? I do keep them private. I've matured to the point where I don't hop up and down or pound my fists on the floor while prostrate. No, I just erupt inwardly, clench my jaw, and glare at people. Perhaps it's similar to being caught in the eye of a hurricane, or more accurately, the "hurricane of an I." Both tempests destroy, whether it be the the landscape or relationships.

Instead of nearly coming apart at the seams, I would rather be welded together more tightly. I'd like a flexible, tempered soul, not a brittle and breakable one.

From the For What It's Worth department, here are several lessons in tempering I've learned—the hard way, of course.

1. "Be ye angry, and sin not: let not the sun go down upon your wrath" (Eph. 4:26). More than once I've considered moving to Nome during the summer, where the sun never sets. In winter I could join the bears in hibernation. Yet, even though they sleep half their lives away, bears have a reputation for grouchiness. I'm afraid I'll have to do my best right here. And I want to stay awake as much as possible so I can watch our family grow and enjoy their activities.

A family can handle short-lived conflicts, but the continual, ongoing types become nasty and divisive. When the sunset spreads its crimson and lavender glory across the horizon, I shall ask God to take any bitterness and rancor I may have, and let it fade away in the gathering dusk.

2. As the Boy Scout motto goes, "Be prepared." My biggest troubles occur when I overreact. I can take a simple disagreement, such as a heated discussion over which TV show to watch, and before I'm done, I've blown it into the proportions of an international incident. If I could learn that I am not duty bound to personally resolve every hiccup in the family, things would probably calm more quickly. I need to be prepared for the inevitable tensions among eight person living under the same roof.

3. There are creative, useful ways to release pent-up emotions. Digging in the garden is an outlet for me, as is shooting baskets through the hoop on the garage. Playing my fiddle is another. Show me a parent who is trying to do a good job, and I'll show you a person who's sometimes tense. Instead of dumping that inner turmoil on others, particularly on your spouse and children, why not direct it toward a helpful target: work in the yard; pick up the family room; get some needed exercise; concentrate on a hobby. Your sense of accomplishment will be a bonus result.

4. When Jacob wrestled all night with the angel, he may have been exhausted, yet he gritted his teeth and said to his opponent, "I will not let thee go, except thou bless me" (Gen. 32:26). I have the same determination concerning family squabbles. We cannot avoid having them now and again. We are able, however, to convert them into blessings, provided we keep them from becoming selfish tantrums and turn them into experiences which temper us.

I much prefer the phrase "molding a child's will" to that of "breaking a child's will." Breaking happens to a hard, unbendable object. But in the case of metals, we apply heat until the metal is in liquid form, add desired alloys and then remold. I don't want my children to have broken wills but malleable ones. Breaking implies a harsh, drastic action; molding involves applying warmth, adding ingredients which temper, and recasting into a new shape.

God grant that children and youth have the property of "meltability," that parents apply the warmth of love, and that our families be tempered with compassion and patience.

"Wherein ye greatly rejoice ... that the trial of your faith, being much more precious than of gold that perisheth, though it be tried with fire, might be found unto praise and honor and glory at the appearing of Jesus Christ" (1 Pet. 1:6, 7).

Twenty-eight

B.C. (BEFORE COMPUTERS)

When I was in high school, I was very proud of my new slide rule. It came complete with a leather case. Fancy. I learned how to multiply, divide, determine square roots and perform other marvelous functions. Of course, I had to round off numbers and make educated guesses.

Strange, I haven't seen a student carrying a slide rule in years. I doubt if high-school students even know what one looks like. With the advent of hand-held calculators, they've become obsolete, relegated to the mathematical museum. A calculator will do everything with precision, displaying numbers to seven decimal places. It does everything except turn itself on. But where's the sense of personal accomplishment and the mystery? I can't argue with those blinkety-blink numbers.

If I wished to control the universe, I'd try to corner the market on 9-volt batteries, because the world is in the grip of power packs, transformers, and batteries. Everybody would be at my beck and call.

It's not easy to keep current with trends, fashions, and the latest electronic gadgets. Video games make me feel like a klutz. Nearly all of them place the player in a crisis situation, demanding lightning-fast reflexes, total recall, and nerves of steel (I'm O for 3). I panic and forget which button controls which blip on the screen.

These so-called games usually put me out of my misery quickly. Quarters and tokens slip rapidly through my fingers.

When I was a child, kids played some marvelous games. A few have survived and can be observed on playgrounds even today: hopscotch, baseball, jacks, and jumping rope. But my favorite exists only in the dim recesses of my memory. Nobody plays marbles anymore! We've got a cardboard box full of them: pee-wees, agates, steelies, clearies and shooters. It warms the cockles of my heart when I stoop to peek inside. They create such a pleasant sound when rolled in one's hand. I've instructed our children in the art and science of marble playing, but to little avail. Maybe if some clever person invented an electric marble, the game would be in style once again.

Everything today is transistorized, computerized, amplified, miniaturized, or remote-controlled. It's hard for me to act knowledgeable when deep down I know how ignorant I am of such things. Perhaps it's enough to take pride in my children's skills and accomplishments. Still, I'd feel better if I had a basic awareness.

Computers are now in use at the grade-school level. Our kids are familiar with the jargon and often use it in mealtime conversations. I hurriedly fill my mouth with food so that to be polite, all I can do is nod my head. That way, I don't give away how naïve I am. The book of Proverbs puts it succinctly: "Even a fool is thought to be wise when he is silent. It pays him to keep his mouth shut" (17:28, TLB).

I want to feel at home in the modern world, but I have a newly-found sympathy for dinosaurs, who, for whatever reason, were unable to adapt to changing conditions. I want to be able to meet the challenges of each new day, to be open to fresh possibilities and opportunities, and to relate to my family in their areas of interest. That's a tall order for a dad who often feels like a grass-hopper in the land of the giants (Num. 13:33).

When I was their age, the big issue for me was whether it was morally right to play "for keeps." I had many long conversations with my parents about this matter, usually after I had won someone else's whole bag of marbles, or had lost my choice ones and was distraught.

Today, the top issues center around how many daily hours of video game playing can be healthy; to what extent does violence on television influence youthful viewers; and the problem of precocious whiz kids prying their home computers into secret government files.

Young people, here's your chance to teach Dad something. I'm at your disposal, though I hope not for your disposal. I'm ready to learn. I've got the calculator mastered. I can make it past level one of several Atari games. And I can correctly use terms like software, on-line, interface, and byte. Well, I can spell them at least. I have no intention (and less ability) of becoming a computer scientist. I'd be thrilled, however, if I could learn enough to operate a word processor. Don't get me wrong, I have much affection for my venerable Royal typewriter. It was originally Grandma Emert's. Ellen learned how to type on its keys. Now, it sits on my desk. There's no question that it has a precious heritage, but perhaps its retirement is in sight. My old slide rule might appreciate a companion on the shelf.

"Give instruction to a wise man, and he will be yet wiser: teach a just man, and he will increase in learning" (Prov. 9:9).

Twenty-nine

APPRECIATING THE ROUGH EDGES

I didn't sleep more than twenty minutes at a stretch last night. Both John and Michael needed to rise early this morning. John's off to a bowling tournament in Omak, and Michael went on a newspaper carrier's trip to a Seattle Seahawks football game. I knew that the alarm was set, but I still kept waking. I didn't dare oversleep. Both boys made their appointments with time to spare. Now in mid-afternoon, I'm yawning as widely as a hungry alligator. If I don't get some coffee in my system soon, I may have to sneak a nap.

Parenting involves many rough edges, lack of sleep being but one minor variety. Others include forever-changing schedules to accommodate children's coming and going; nothing ever staying clean and in its proper place; having only a dollar or two in your billfold or purse except on the day you're paid; and sitting on hard, steel benches at a son's football games. The hardness wouldn't be so bad if they weren't also cold and damp. No matter how much I bundle up, the frigid wind finds a way to chill me. How cheerleaders can endure a game in their short skirts is more than I can figure. Maybe that's why they are studies in perpetual motion.

Speaking of rough edges, I must mention bread crusts. Left-over crusts on a plate upset me. Eating all the soft bread and leaving the crust perfectly intact is a disgusting skill. I'm partial to heels, so I don't understand why the kids work so hard at it. Anyway, I put my parental foot down. "Crusts are the best part of the loaf and have the most nutrition." I'm not certain that's the whole truth, but it makes a good story. David is the only one who likes end pieces best. He's a young man after my own heart—or stomach.

Roughage is critical for good nutrition, and vegetable skins are valuable sources of vitamins. So what do we do? We peel off the outer coverings and cook the life out of the vegetables. Then we beat it smooth so it's easy to eat and digest. We destroy a lot of the food value.

Right after Christmas last year, our television set went on the fritz. Horror! It was going to be a rough vacation without the TV. How could we fix it or replace it? We had spent all our money. Actually, the word "all" is inaccurate. There was never that much in the first place. Anyway, the TV was making squiggly lines and going blank. The children were aghast. The prospect of no television was more than they could handle. I was admittedly concerned: first, with the financial burden of purchasing a new set; and secondly, with the specter of missing football games on New Year's Day.

However, I also nurtured a secret joy. A wonderful and blessed peace had blossomed in our home. No one was arguing about which show to watch. There was no prying them away from the screen when bedtime rolled around. They were busying themselves with creative, active things.

The old set proved durable; it revived. They got to see their favorite programs and I watched football until I became bleary-eyed.

Do we do the same thing with life? We become upset at the prospect of no television; we refuse to eat the crusts; we try to avoid roughage; we strive for comfort and ease. In the process, we grow soft and complacent. I worry that we aren't producing enough pioneer characters today. I mean the old-fashioned type who were of hardy stock, rough, tough and resilient, able to keep going in great adversity. The pioneers didn't have to have it the easy way; they adjusted and survived.

In our neck of the woods, apple trees are the big item. Orchards abound. Our Chamber of Commerce rather immodestly advertises our city as the "Apple Capital of the World." Humility takes a backseat when it comes to making money. I've been told by experts that this area consistently produces high quality apples because the trees have to struggle. Winters get cold and water is at a premium. The trees concentrate on producing fruit and not on growing lush foliage. There's no time for looking good. All resources must be focused on the significant task of yielding a crop. Like the apple tree, perhaps we can learn to appreciate life's rough edges, and can use them to help us bear good fruit, fruit which abides.

I am very thankful that centuries ago one person chose not to take the easy way out. Jesus was willing to endure the rough edges of a rugged cross. That event has made all the difference in our lives. He has called us to take up our cross and to follow.

"Lord, help me accept and appreciate the rough edges."

"For I reckon that the sufferings of this present time are not worthy to be compared with the glory which shall be revealed in us" (Rom. 8:18).

Thirty

SPARE TIME, EXTRA CASH AND OTHER MYTHS

Maybe I'll learn someday. I plan too many projects and attempt more work than humanly can be done in the available time. When I have a day at home, I'm usually a bit weary from my ministerial duties, but that doesn't stop me from overscheduling. I've got a hundred things to do around the house: mow the lawn (the shag look is permissible only for carpets); change the oil and filter on the car; help Ellen defrost the freezer (I can't imagine why, the frost is only three inches thick and the door almost closes); go shopping for David's upcoming birthday; dash to the bank and post office; write a clever, scintillating chapter for my next book (don't I wish); enjoy a leisurely lunch with Ellen; and take a nap. Except I cannot relax. Everything seems to take longer than I anticipated. The day is nearly gone and I have 97 unfinished (unstarted) jobs.

Frustration rears its homely head. I wish for once I'd set more modest goals and better estimate my abilities and energy. Eventually it all gets done. However, I'd eliminate a great deal of tension if I were more realistic and scaled down my expectations. The unvarnished truth is that spare time is a scarce commodity. No one hands it to me on a silver platter. I must seek after it and firmly stake my claim to it. Otherwise, family and friends will find uses aplenty for it.

I cherish and nurture a dream (call it a fantasy if you like) of a day in the sweet by-and-by when I'll have time to unhurriedly complete every task. There'll be no pressure from within or without. I'll be free from the incessant demands of the clock.

I realize that such a condition will never happen in this life. I observe Grandma and Grandpa who retired from active employment a decade ago; they're busier now than ever. Stress is an ever-present reality in their lives. The sources may be different for them than for me, but the emotional results are the same.

I do my best dreaming while brewing in the bathtub. Until we can afford a hot tub, I'll just have to slide down and get as much of my body submerged as possible. I fantasize about the royalties from selling millions of books. Then I'm off to a forest primeval, beside a gurgling brook. A rustic log cabin sits at the edge of a flower-carpeted meadow with fir trees rising majestically behind. Total peace. I'm at one with creation and its Creator.

Reality often crashes in abruptly upon my reverie. "Dad, how long does it take you to get clean? I need to get in the bathroom—quick." They just don't understand. Clean has little or nothing to do with it.

Would that time were the only resource in short supply. For instance, there is a shortage of handy answers to the tough questions children ask:

"Dad, how come cats kill birds? It's not because they're hungry. And besides, birds are so cute."

"What causes lightning and thunder?"

"Will there be a nuclear war?"

"If you get fired, what would happen to us?"

Some of the hardest questions are seldom asked aloud. They lurk just over the horizon, awaiting that moment when I feel most inadequate.

Another resource consistently in short supply is money. We carefully allocate our funds and it appears they'll cover all the bases. Bingo! Up jumps an emergency. I wouldn't mind emergencies so much if they weren't always expensive. Back to the dining room table we go. We spread out the bills, calculate our income sources (the "for sures," our "hope so's," and our "probably not's"), and redesign a fiscal strategy.

The only predictable thing about family finances is their un-predictability. Amy's dental retainer breaks. Steve loses his one good sweatshirt. Sara is invited to a birthday party and needs to bring a gift. John needs $30 for a debate trip. David's bicycle tire goes flat. Mike can't wear jeans to the orchestra concert, so we must buy a pair of dark dress pants. My typewriter needs a new ribbon, and I have two luncheon meetings at which my presence is required. As if this weren't enough, Sara runs proudly home from school with news she's lost a tooth. Even that costs money. While the tooth fairy program may be a nice idea, it has never received any government grants. It comes out of Ellen's or my pocket. When I go to lunch, I hope the waitress understands. Her tip went to a gap-toothed daughter.

The last time Sara had a tooth fall out, she lost it. Panic. There was no visible proof for the tooth fairy. Our particular fairy pays about 75¢ per molar—I'm curious to know if this is close to the national tooth fairy average. Ellen wrote a note to verify Sara's claim, and next morning Sara found her coins inside the large stuffed tooth that hung on her doorknob.

Spare time, extra cash, magic answers, sleeping in on Saturday mornings, and uninterrupted evenings at home; these must all be figments of my imagination. Nevertheless, I'm going to keep hoping. Someday, maybe, perhaps . . .

"For we are saved by hope: but hope that is seen is not hope: for what a man seeth, why doth he yet hope for?" (Rom. 8:24).

Thirty-one

LIVING AGAIN AFTER DYING OF EMBARRASSMENT

I was raised by incredibly patient parents. They endured my antics and suffered through my occasionally rebellious behavior. I vividly remember a Sunday morning worship service in which I caused my preacher father great anguish and embarrassment. I was sitting at the back of the sanctuary with several of my seventh-grade buddies. My usual activities were doodling, making paper airplanes, and stage-voice whispering.

Our antics escalated on this particular Sabbath. I had borrowed the matches used for lighting the altar candles, and halfway through my dad's sermon, I set a bulletin on fire. I didn't intend for it to burn furiously, but the smoke poured up as I frantically stamped out the flames. Father stepped out of the pulpit, looked straight at me, and in no uncertain terms told me to quit playing with matches. Then, addressing the congregation, he apologized. "This is most embarrassing for me, but rest assured, the appropriate action will be taken." I would have been embarrassed, too, had I not been so scared.

Father and son lived to tell about the episode. Our faces no doubt reddened, but their normal color soon returned. Fortunately, from my back row vantage point, I could not see my mother's expression. My parents did remain in that parish for several

120

more years and had a fruitful ministry. And from that event I learned two important lessons: don't cause trouble when your dad's preaching; and (as I stand in the pulpit) keep your eye on activity in the back pews.

We all experience embarrassment; we're fallible human creatures. My latest humbling experience was learning to ski. I seemed to slide more on my backside than on the skis. I finally stopped looking to see who might be watching, and discovered that most people didn't seem to notice or even care. They were busy trying to stay upright themselves. I now swoosh along quite smoothly. I fall once in a while, but snow provides a soft cushion and brushes off easily. Happily, no one can tell if the blush on my cheeks is from embarrassment or the cold air.

It's hard for most of us to admit our mistakes and errors. A youngster with his hand in the cookie jar may say something like, "Oh, is this the cookie jar? I thought it was the soap dish." I wasn't born yesterday, or even the day before yesterday. We both know that we both know the truth. But the explanation, lame though it be, enables him to save face.

Face-saving may be all right. Heart protecting is not. In other words, it's not sinful to act happy-go-lucky or nonchalant in the midst of embarrassment. The expression today is "act cool." When that coolness penetrates the heart, however, barriers are built. Act cool, if you must, but keep your heart warm and soft and loving.

Every Monday afternoon, Ellen and I throw ourselves into a potentially embarrassing situation. We deliver the *Wenatchee World* newspaper. It's our second stint. John was a paperboy several years ago, and now Michael is one. Both learned the virtues of reliability, promptness, and financial record keeping, the last with Ellen's guidance. When John was away at church camp, or sick, or turning out for school sports, Ellen and I filled in. I had never delivered papers as a boy, so I viewed it as a challenge. I could roll and rubber band the pile of ninety papers in fifteen minutes. It took almost as long to wash the black smudges off my fingers.

Of course, we heard many snide remarks. "My, my, aren't you a cute paperboy."

"How much does he pay you for being his assistants?"

"Whose route is this, yours or his?"

John did the bulk of the work; so does Michael. Monday, though, is his piano lesson. So Ellen and I deliver the papers. It's good exercise, provides lots of fresh air, and gives us a chance to visit with each other. I do wonder what folks along the route think of us.

The other day, Michael had a dentist appointment which ran late. I stuffed my coat pockets with sugar cookies and started out to deliver the papers in a pouring rain. The cookies were my reward for being such a good daddy. What a sight I must have been! I was dripping wet with a soggy newspaper bag draped across my shoulders, and munching cookies and looking confused. I missed one subscriber. When I finally remembered my mistake, I had to backtrack to correct it. Then I slogged home to dry out and enjoy one more cookie. I was certain it wouldn't spoil my appetite for dinner.

I like to think there's nothing much about me to cause embarrassment. I'm just a unique individual who skips along to the cadence of a different drummer. It helps that through the years I've learned to laugh at myself and my predicaments. I still know how to blush, but I guess that's part of my charm.

"For I have learned, in whatsoever state I am, therewith to be content. I know both how to be abased, and I know how to abound..." (Phil. 4:11b, 12a).

Thirty-two

EVERYTHING KIDS WANT TO TELL PARENTS BUT ARE AFRAID OF BEING SPANKED FOR

I have recently made a special effort to listen to what our children have to say to us, their parents—not only the compliments or the superficial remarks, but the deeply honest and difficult-to-say things. I write this chapter in the hope that other parents will be motivated to listen carefully to their children's thoughts and feelings. I have arranged my findings in a series of "Dear Dad" letters.

Dear Dad,

I know you try, but sometimes you don't hear what I'm saying. Maybe you just get so wrapped up in your work or in what you've got to do, that you don't listen. Oh, sure, you look right at me and nod your head, but I can tell when your mind is wandering. I know I take too long to tell my stories and that I tell them at the wrong time, when you're super busy. You're tired after a long day at work. But I get tired, too. Maybe some stuff doesn't seem as exciting to you as it does to me, like a gold star or an "A" on a paper; learning how to write cursive; doing the best at jumping rope during recess; or seeing a fuzzy caterpillar on the way home from school.

It's important to me that you really hear and understand
and care. I want to be able to tell you how I feel when
I'm happy and when I'm sad. You don't have to know
all the answers. If you're there when I need you and
will give me your undivided attention, that's what
counts.

Dear Dad,

Don't blame yourself for my moods. I'm not going to
be happy all the time, any more than you are. When I
pout, it's probably not your fault, even if I yell at you
and make you feel guilty. And don't take everything
I say personally, especially when I'm mad. Let me say
dumb things just like you and Mom do sometimes. When
I slam my bedroom door in a huff because I'm upset,
please don't slam the door of your heart. I'll come out
pretty soon. I may scowl, stare daggers, and grump
around. Let me be a not-yet-grown-up person. Let me
feel the whole range of emotions. I'll eventually mature
if you'll be patient with me.

Dear Dad,

Could you stop answering all my requests with "Yes,
but...!"? I ask to go somewhere, and you reply, "Well, I
guess it's all right, but ..." Then you add a bunch of
conditions: "But you'd better be back in an hour; but
you shouldn't spend too much money; but don't hang
around with so-and-so; but have you finished your
homework?" I don't mind your checking on me. As a
matter of fact, it feels good to know you care. But just
once I wish you'd say, "Yes—period." That would be
a pleasant surprise!

Dear Dad,

Give me room to grow. My body needs more and
more space as I develop physically. Well, give my mind
and heart some room, too. I need your support, that's

for sure. But don't crowd me. I want you to encourage and nudge me gently, not steamroll me. I'm going to make mistakes, probably as many as you made. Don't rush in to correct everything. Let me learn from my errors. Give me lots of advice without nagging me; encourage me without pushing me; set limits but don't imprison me. I *want* you to offer guidelines. I really do not want to rebel, contrary to what it must seem to you at times. When I feel you're boxing me in, I start squirming. Support me; don't suffocate me. Go with me but don't do it all for me. You may find this hard to believe, but I don't even want you to give me everything I ask for. I actually like hearing you say no, if you say it kindly and explain your reasons.

Dear Dad,

You don't have to be "with it" all the time. I don't care whether you know our latest slang. You've got enough to do following world events and keeping track of business trends. Anyhow, as soon as you learn what our words mean, we have to change them. We like slang because it's our private language. And you don't have to appreciate the music I listen to, or wear your hair in today's style. Be the old fuddy duddy you are. You can be interested in all the fashion stuff if you like, but let me be the one who wears it.

Dear Dad,

Keep your chin up (or should I say chins). You'll make it. I know you can do it. We know it's tough to be a parent in the world today, with lots of problems and pressures. Hang in there, Pop. We'll help you as much as we can. After all, we have a big stake in your success. Good luck, and God bless.

"But speaking the truth in love, may [we] grow up into him in all things, which is the head, even Christ" (Eph. 4:15).

Thirty-three

TO WAIT UP OR NOT TO WAIT UP

John had left for work at 6 p.m. to make pizza dough, pile on mozzarella cheese, and pour tomato sauce. Meanwhile, back at the house we were busy with preparations for the first day of school—baths, curlers, new clothes laid out, pencils sharpened, and lunch sacks ready on the kitchen counter. It was "early to bed" because morning would be "early to rise."

By 9:30 they were cleanly, neatly tucked in bed. Ellen and I settled back, snacked on leftovers from dinner, watched television, and waited for John to arrive home. Soon after the eleven o'clock news, weariness overtook us. We brushed our teeth and retired, planning to listen for John.

I sat up in bed with a start and looked at the clock: 1:30 a.m. Our dozing had turned to snoring. John was not home. The blue Fiat was not parked in the driveway.

I paced about nervously. "Where is that boy? He should have been home long ago. The restaurant closes at eleven. Has he had car trouble? An accident?" Finally, I hopped in our other car and drove by the pizza place. There in the parking lot sat our little blue car. Back home again, I debated whether or not to call and check on him. *He's a young man of seventeen, usually quite responsible. How will it sound if I call and tell the manager to please send our little boy home because it's past his bedtime?* I was torn between wanting John safely in his room and embarrassing him before fellow workers.

By 3:00 a.m. I no longer cared about whom I embarrassed. I telephoned. Ellen and I were still awake when he tiptoed in the door at 4:00. I resisted the urge to lecture him with, "This had better not happen again on a school night. You need your sleep. I hope you can stay alert in class tomorrow—oops, I mean today." He literally fell into bed; slept for three hours, and then groggily left to begin his senior year. He survived it better than his parents did and worked late again the next night. We were exhausted.

To wait up or not to wait up, that is the question. We do trust them. They're super kids, capable and possessing good judgment. Yet, they are not fully grown and they're still under our legal care. I know John is an excellent driver. He would not knowingly, intentionally get into trouble. But what if it were someone else's fault? I have an active imagination which goes into overdrive in the middle of the night when loved ones aren't where I think they're supposed to be.

Ellen was extra late returning from an art class one cold, dreary evening. Freezing rain was gradually spreading a coat of ice on the roadways. By the time she finally arrived home, I had visualized the car at the bottom of a ravine, smashed against a concrete abutment, overturned at the base of a steep hill, and Ellen trapped beneath the wreck. Rather inventive, don't you think? In reality, the gals in the group had been visiting, and one of them had brought dessert.

What happened next is what often happens next. My anxiety turned to anger. What had thus far produced inner fretting now had an actual person in focus. "Where in the world have you been?" My voice had an accusing tone. "I've been sitting here worried to pieces. The least you could have done was call and let me know you'd be late." I love people enough to get mad once in a while. And, thank God, they still love me when I do.

I love my kids enough to let go of them when it's necessary, to give them room to explore, to make their own discoveries, and enjoy adventures. How will they learn more than the old folks if they are never out of our sight? One of the greatest hopes for the future is that our young people will have access to learning tools we didn't have, and gain deeper understanding about our world.

If we bind them to our traditions, they may also repeat our mistakes. Tying children to the "apron strings" is not conducive to their development. Anyway, have you ever tried to move quickly with a big teenager tied to your apron strings? It's cumbersome for both of you. We fathers may not wear aprons very often, but don't let that fool you. We have our methods of holding on.

How can they mature if we refuse to trust them when they prove deserving of it? This fall, for example, Steve had his heart set on buying a moped. He'd saved money from his summer job. I wasn't convinced it was a good idea—"What if he has an acccident?" I waffled but eventually yielded when I decided it was preferable to a full-fledged motorcycle. Then Steve talked me into taking it out for a spin by myself. It was scary for an old man who'd never been on anything racier than a scooter or a wobbly three-speed. I prayed the whole time (with eyes wide open), "Lord, don't let me crash." I didn't, but I did have to figure out how to dismount gracefully.

Sometimes children need holding and hugging and lap-sitting. Other times, they need parents who look the other way, or who cover their eyes with their fingers. I hope it's okay if I peek once in a while.

"And give unto ... my son a perfect heart, to keep thy commandments, thy testimonies, and thy statutes..." (1 Chron. 29:19).

Thirty-four

BLEST BE THE BINDS THAT TIE

We have some great times of family fellowship, many experiences where joy flows freely. I'm truly thankful for the happy moments and that they outnumber the sad ones. But over the years I've come to realize an important fact. Though happy moments are nice, what really holds us together are the scrapes we get into, and out of, and the difficulties we survive. I appreciate days of peace and calm when nothing intrudes on our carefully established routine. Let me assure you, I do not go looking for troubles. But I will not try to keep my family from dealing with them, for we get stronger as we struggle to overcome adversity.

A favorite Gospel hymn expresses a profound truth: "Blest Be the Tie That Binds." Permit me to tamper with this venerable title by transposing two words. Pretend it reads, "Blest Be the Binds That Tie." Our family gets into enough binds that if we cannot find a blessing in their midst, it would be depressing indeed. Ah, but binds are God's blessings dressed in work clothes. Even the binds and tight spots "work together for good to them that love God" (Rom. 8:28).

An analogy might be drawn by examining a brick wall. When I look at it, I see only bricks; my eyes don't focus on the mortar unless my mind instructs them to do so. Yet without the cement, the bricks would simply lie stacked in piles, waiting to be used.

131

The binds we encounter are a valuable ingredient in the mortar of family life. Certainly, a family shouldn't concentrate on the problems. Yet, they are a part of every relationship, and when dealt with creatively, they strengthen the mortar that holds us together.

Sara, our four-year-old, watched with fascination as Ellen cut her brothers' hair. So the next day, while eight-year-old Amy was in school, she decided to give big sister's favorite doll a haircut. After all, it had made her brothers cuter. The doll was less fortunate. Sara was overcome with remorse, and worried about possible revenge—Amy had a temper to match her red hair. Three o'clock and Amy arrived at precisely the same moment. Tension filled the kitchen as she helped herself to a snack. Our theory was that a child stuffed with graham crackers and peanut butter is less likely to explode.

Ellen began, "By the way, Amy, we had this little accident today." Long pause. The crunching of crackers continued unabated. "Sara wanted to make your doll look prettier." Long pause number two. More graham crackers. "She gave it a haircut." Ellen produced the doll from behind her back. We braced as if we'd just lighted a giant firecracker and the "bang!" was imminent.

But no "bang," not even a "pop." Amy smiled and gently, lovingly received her doll. She was not the least bit upset. The double allotment of crackers probably hadn't hurt, but that didn't explain her reaction. We had forgotten a quality of children: they judge by inner realities and not by outward appearances. We saw a mangled, ugly doll. She saw a doll she had loved for years, and she still loved it. She may have loved it even more now in its pathetic state. Sara visibly relaxed and approached Amy seeking reconciliation. They hugged and all was forgiven. Two young girls were drawn together more closely as sisters. Blest be the binds that tie!

A common bind for most families is a shortage of funds. Though it causes short-term anxiety, I have found it to be a source of long-term joy. I seldom appreciate a lack of money during our short times. But in looking back, I recall how close we felt to one another as we scrimped and sacrificed. For example, Ellen and I were students in Boston shortly after our marriage. We both worked part time and much of our meager income was gobbled up by tuition, books, and typing paper. Our special treat was to get ice cream cones at a shop about three blocks away. One evening we collected all our pennies, finding the last few by digging in the creases of an overstuffed chair. We splurged and ordered "jimmies" (chocolate sprinkles on top). To our chagrin, the price had jumped five cents since our last trip, but our forlorn looks must have made the attendant take pity on us. My, they tasted delicious! Over twenty years' worth of ice cream has since slid down my throat, but none has compared to the cone I licked as we walked hand in hand down Commonwealth Avenue on a warm summer evening.

Grandma Groseclose became seriously ill last fall. Initially brought about by a potassium deficiency, her condition worsened with vertebrae fracturing in her lower back. In severe pain, she could barely breathe, let alone move. Grandpa was a marvelous helpmate. Our family responded as best we knew how. Grandchildren made get-well gifts. We arranged flowers from our garden, gave her a music box that played a lively tune, and visited her often.

Following one lengthy hospital stay, she stopped by our house briefly before going home. Walking was difficult for her, so, since she weighed less than ninety pounds, I simply picked her up and carried her in my arms. My emotions surged as I realized how the cycle had come around. She who had carried me was now in my arms. The lump in my throat refused to go away when I swallowed. Grandma's physical infirmities had drawn us together. We remembered her constantly in our prayers. We called frequently. We wish a total recovery for her, yet we give thanks for the way in which such a bind ties us together in Christian love.

We are bound together by legal, historical, and financial ties. But strangely, marvelously, we are also tied together by the binds into which we get. Hallelujah!

"And not only so, but we glory in tribulations also: knowing

that tribulation worketh patience; and patience, experience; and experience, hope: and hope maketh not ashamed; because the love of God is shed abroad in our hearts by the Holy Ghost which is given unto us" (Rom. 5:3–5).

Thirty-five

ALL IN THE FOLD

Just a typical Friday evening. John had finished work at God-father's Pizza, then dropped by the bowling alley to hang around. Steve was a hundred miles away playing in a high-school football game. Amy had a baby-sitting job halfway across town. The three youngest children were visiting their cousins, Danny and Jill. Ellen and I sat at home, a mixture of feelings. We were delighted by the peace and calm. But like the settlers of the last century, we felt it was too quiet. When we're accustomed to a full nest and flying feathers, there's a loneliness that creeps in when it's empty and silent.

"I wonder how John's work is going?"

"If Amy has any trouble, I'm sure she'll call."

"I hope Steve has a good game and doesn't get hurt."

"Did Uncle Frank say he was bringing the kids home, or are we supposed to go get them?"

A vague uneasiness hung over our house. When Uncle Frank brought the three home at 10 p.m., we relaxed a bit. Amy returned from baby-sitting at 11. Soon after midnight, I heard the ta-pock-etta of our old car rounding the corner. John was back. Ellen and I went to bed, leaving a window partly open (we like fresh air). But it was hard to sleep soundly with cars driving past. Finally, I heard a rumble that had to be Jeff's pickup truck (Jeff is Steve's football buddy). I listened as Steve quietly entered the house and made a beeline to the refrigerator, then to the bathroom and to bed. *Now* we could relax, all the way down to our toes. I could quit listening and concentrate on sleeping.

I know a little how the shepherd must have felt when his one sheep was lost (Luke 15). The ninety-nine were safely in the fold. But one precious animal was missing. When one of our children is gone, there's a feeling of incompleteness. Yes, there are still seven of us gathered at the dinner table. However, a special somebody isn't in his appointed place. There is no noticeable decrease in noise; the chewing and talking are just as loud as usual. Yet, I feel a loneliness tucked in a corner of my heart.

I observed that same feeling in ten-year-old Sara's eyes the other day. Big brother John is a senior this year and has been receiving letters from universities far and wide. During the evening meal we were discussing which campuses appealed most to him. When 3000-mile-away Boston University was mentioned, Sara looked sad, wistful. "I don't want John to leave, not ever. Can't we always be together?"

The answer, Sara, is no and yes. No, we cannot remain forever as we are, in our cozy little bungalow. Each of the children will continue to grow; will be educated in another community or state; will marry a person from a different part of the country; will choose a profession that takes him or her to some corner of the globe. Geography is certain to separate some, if not most, of us. Yet the answer, Sara, is also yes. Once a family, always a family. Ellen and I will never stop loving them, no matter how far away they may be. In a very real sense, they'll never be "on their own." Our care and support will go with them as long as we all live.

It's a pleasant feeling when all tribal members are within our house. We know precisely where they are. They're "all present and accounted for." In a moment of exasperation, we may express a desire to be temporarily rid of one or more of them—that's simply a safety-valve expression. It's a very secure feeling to have them all in the fold.

We no longer tuck older ones in bed, except in jest or good fun. They'd probably be embarrassed and so would we. Anyway, to accomplish that, the "tucker" must stay up later than the "tuckee." Night owl John would never get his share.

Perhaps this gives us a glimpse into the ways of God. Does He receive satisfaction when all His precious children are safe and sound, when they're all in the fold and the Shepherd is guarding them? The Lord most certainly notices when someone is lost or has strayed. So do we human parents. It's an important part of the work we do.

It's 9:45 p.m. right now. I'm listening again. John's due back from a debate tournament. Steve's soon supposed to be home from a movie. Amy should have been here thirty minutes ago from studying with her friend Patty. It's an average night for us. At least Mike, Sara and David are in bed—well, almost. You wouldn't believe how they can prolong bedtime preparations.

I can hardly wait until they're all in the fold. Then I can perform my one final duty: tuck myself in.

"He shall feed his flock like a shepherd: he shall gather the lambs with his arms, and carry them in his bosom, and shall gently lead those that are with young" (Isa. 40:11).

Thirty-six

A FATHER'S VERSION OF 1 CORINTHIANS 13

If I obey the latest book on child-rearing, and speak always to my children calmly and with sweetness, but have not love, our home is cold and barren. If I understand child psychology and have mastered all methods of discipline, and if I have lots of energy so as to perform the mountains of work required, but have not love, I am not a good parent. If I spend all my waking hours doing things for them, give them everything they want, and run to their activities until I am literally burned out, but have not love, I have accomplished nothing.

Love is patient and kind, and smiles while cleaning up messes. Love is not jealous when children demand time, nor does it boastfully say, "When I was your age, I did such and such." Parental love is not based on being the biggest or making the most money. It does not insist on its own way. Just because I'm tired doesn't mean the children must stay out of my way or go to bed. Such love is not irritable; it is not resentful and it quickly forgets the mistakes children make. It does not remember the words they utter in a moment of anger. Love does not rejoice when any child or youth gets into trouble, but rejoices when a family dwells together in harmony.

Love can stand slumber parties, loud music, and mud on freshly-waxed kitchen floors. Love believes in children's potential for growth, and expects the best of them. Love hopes that children will become compassionate, caring, and productive citizens. Love endures all things: grief over a dead parakeet, "F's" on report cards, waiting up and worrying until 2 a.m., maximum lines of credit of MasterCard, and much more.

So faith, hope, love abide, these three; but the greatest of these is love.